Someone Paved The Way

Sylvia Johnson-Cooper, Ph.D.

Roosevelt Flenard, WWII Sailor

Bloomington, IN Milton Keynes, UK

AuthorHouse™ *AuthorHouse™ UK Ltd.*
1663 Liberty Drive, Suite 200 *500 Avebury Boulevard*
Bloomington, IN 47403 *Central Milton Keynes, MK9 2BE*
www.authorhouse.com *www.authorhouse.co.uk*
Phone: 1-800-839-8640 *Phone: 08001974150*

© 2006 Sylvia Johnson-Cooper, Ph.D.. All rights reserved.

*No part of this book may be reproduced, stored in
a retrieval system, or transmitted by any means
without the written permission of the author.*

First published by AuthorHouse 12/20/2006

ISBN: 978-1-4259-7003-1 (sc)

*Printed in the United States of America
Bloomington, Indiana*

This book is printed on acid-free paper.

Hello Peg   5-2-08

Much love + luck to and family.
Best wishes to you and family. May God Bless you and your family and may they have a long life.
(Roosevelt Fleurd "Rosey")

DEDICATION

This book is dedicated to mothers for keeping their children on the straight and narrow, although it may be difficult.

THE BRAVEST BATTLE

The bravest battle that ever was fought!
Shall I tell you where and when?
On the maps of the world you will find it not;
It was fought by the mothers of men.

Nay, not with cannon or battle-shot,
With a sword or noble pen;
Nay, not with eloquent words or thought
From mouths of wonderful men!

But deep in a walled-up woman's heart –
Of a woman that would not yield,
But bravely, silently bore her part –
Lo, there is that battlefield!

No marshaling troops, no bivouac song,
No banner to gleam and wave;
But oh! These battles, they last so long –
From babyhood to the grave.

Yet, faithful still as a bridge of stars,
She fights in her walled-up town –
Fights on and on in the endless wars,
Then, silent, unseen, goes down.

Oh, ye with banners and battle-shot,
    And soldiers to shout and praise!
I tell you the kingliest victories fought
    Were fought in those silent ways.

O spotless woman in a world of shame,
    With splendid and silent scorn,
Go back to God as white as you came –
    The kingliest warrior born!

Written by Joaquin Miller.

IN MEMORY
Virgie Robinett Johnson -
January 15, 1913 – December 15, 1990

MY MOTHER

by Frederic Hentz Adams

She was as good as goodness is,
Her acts and all her words were kind,
And high above all memories
I hold the beauty of her mind.

Love,
Sylvia

IN MEMORY
Margie Grant Mitchell –
March 6, 1902 – March 31, 1989

MY BOY

by Charles C. Wakefield

"So let him live,
Love work, love play,
Love all that life can give;
And when he grows too weary to feel joy,
Leave life, with laughter, to some other boy."

Love,
Rosy

ACKNOWLEDGEMENT

Special thanks to my sons, Kerry and Horace, my three grandchildren, Jayme Leigh, Rachel Lois, and Kerry Reyes, for their care and love while I was writing this with Rosy Flenard.

I am extremely grateful to my sister Lourene Johnson Medlow for her editing and giving me positive feedback about this story about "Rosy", although at times, I know she thought I did not want it. I did. Thank you!

PREFACE

The depression of the early 30's, 1930 – 1932, was tough, but President Franklin D. Roosevelt put young men to work everywhere he could including in the armed forces to keep the country moving. It was especially hard for African-Americans, because jobs were so scarce, and African-Americans were not allowed to enlist in the armed forces. It was 1936 before the president opened up the Army and Navy (CC camp, NYA, NRA, WPA) to African-Americans.

Filipino and Chinese males were already in the Navy and the few African-Americans that stayed in from World War I. Secretary of Navy said he would permit African-Americans to come into the Navy at this time, but as mess attendants only: serving tables, shinning shoes, and etc.

The Navy began a recruiting program. A few African-Americans were selected: those with high school education and college degrees. Just as the Secretary of Navy said, regardless to education, skill, or trade, African-Americans came into the Navy as mess attendants only.

From 1940 to 1942, more African-Americans came into the Navy than ever before because more ships were being commissioned, therefore, there was a need for more mess attendants. But it was a year later after the war started in 1942, before the Navy opened its door to African-American mid-shipmen at the Naval Academy.

The mid-shipmen cruises that I participated in, did not have any African-Americans; however, records from the US Naval Academy Alumni Association Maryland, reports that Lieutenant Commander Wesley A. Brown, USN (retired), Class of 1949, was the first African-American mid-shipman to graduate from the Naval Academy. It is not known the total number of African-Americans that entered the Naval Academy, and for reason unknown were drummed out.

On December 7, 1941, at Pearl Harbor, Dorie Miller manned a 50 cal machine gun and shot down Japanese planes. This proves that if African-Americans had been given the training like any other white sailor, the Navy for African-Americans would have been better. However, mess attendants were all the Navy had to offer African-Americans; even that we did our best.

To all the African-American admirals, captains, commanders, and other officers in the United States Navy that are making a career in the Navy, many, many young African-Americans seeking the same opportunity were denied, because of their race. Those that rose to greatness, can look back at the thousands who were not fortunate, and be thankful that someone paved the way for them.

Roosevelt Flenard
August 2006

ROSY FLENARD
Chapter 1

> *"Today will never happen again. Don't waste it with a false start or no start at all. You were not born to fail."*
>
> Og Mandino

When I was about five years old, my mother carried me down to the ship channel to see one of the United States Navy's war-ship that was in the Port of Houston. I remember going aboard, and walking around the deck looking at such a huge ship. I also remember that one tall white sailor with bell bottom pants and a tight fitting jumper, a blue or black flat hat, bent over and shook my hand. He pointed out the guns, boats, and revealed other parts of the ship to me that I can no longer remember.

As I grew up, I always remembered that event: going on that Navy war-ship. Every time I went to Galveston, I was interested in going down to see the ships. This inspired me to want to join the Navy. Some years later, a class mate of mine went into the Navy; and he came home on leave, all decked out in his uniform, furthered inspired me to go into the Navy.

In May 1938, I finished high school, and my chance of going to college was out, because my dad died three years earlier, and my mother could not afford to send me. I wanted to go into the Navy then, but first I tried earning money for college but to no avail. So early April 1939, I went to the Navy recruiting office and signed up.

After signing up for the Navy, I told my mother "No you didn't, Rosy", was her reply. I was eighteen and I did not need her permission to sign up. She said, "There is a war going on in Europe. You don't know anything about fighting. Anyway you are too little; they won't take you", she added. She went on like this for awhile, but I paid her no mind. My mind was made up.

Whether I was small or big, I wanted to be part of the Navy. That had always been my dream: to sail the ocean blue and serve my country. I left for work with her still fussing about the Navy. I delivered prescriptions and other items for a drug store. She was still fussing when I returned home after work.

The recruiting man came to the house to tell her I enlisted in the Navy and how good it was for me because I would get a chance to travel, and see the world, good insurance, food, and clothing, to say the least about the Navy being very educational. My mother interrupted with, "And Hitler will get my baby." He said, "Miss, Hitler won't get him; we are not at war." She interrupted again, "You soon will be." The recruiter got fluster and shot back, "Miss, your son is 18 and parents' signatures are not required." But no sooner said than he was sorry for it. He then tried to assure her that I would be alright and the Navy would take good care of me. But my mother would not hear any of it. She did not want me to go. I was her baby, only baby, all 140 pounds of me. He finally said good day and left. She fussed some more but not as much, maybe because she got a better understanding of the Navy, or maybe, she knew I was going anyway without her permission.

Before I received a letter from the Navy telling me where to report, my mother gave me her blessing. I was to report to the Naval recruiting office in downtown Houston at 9:00 A.M., Monday, September 18, 1939.

I didn't get into the Navy before September because the Navy department changed the enlistment from four years to six years, and finalization of some personal papers. These two problems slowed the process of enlistment; however, I was accepted and so thankful. I shouted, "U.S. Navy here I come!"

I was known as "Rosy", which is short for Roosevelt, to my family and friends, but not to my Navy's buddies. I was just plain Flenard to them.

NAVY BOOT CAMP
Chapter 2

"Each morning the day lays like a fresh shirt on our bed...The happiness of the next 24 hours depends on our ability, on waking, to pick it up."

Walter Benjamin

My name is Roosevelt Flenard, Serial Number 3600613, Rate Matt 3/C. I was employed by the United States Navy for six years with a beginning pay of $21.00 per month. I began my enlistment in the United States Navy on September 18, 1939, in Houston, Texas, along with three other black fellows named Perry, Benson, and Smith, from different parts of Texas. I was eighteen years old.

I reported to the naval office as I was told to do. I was examined, and then I signed a bunch of papers. At lunch time, one of the recruiters took me and the other fellows over to the restaurant across from the post office to eat. In the restaurant, we were seated in the rear, behind a curtain. The recruiter returned to his office. He returned for us about thirty minutes later after we had lunch.

The fellows and I returned to finish up signing papers. We finished around four. However, the train that we were to ride to Virginia did not leave until nine that night. So the recruiter entrusted me with the four railroad tickets, meal tickets, and Pullman tickets from Houston to Norfolk, Virginia, because I was from Houston and I knew my way around the city. I took the three fellows home to meet my mother and we hung out until it was time to board the train that night at nine.

The four of us left Houston that Monday night heading for boot camp in Norfolk, Virginia. We changed trains in St. Louis, and several other African-American Navy recruits boarded the train. We left St. Louis, arriving in Cincinnati, Ohio, early Tuesday evening. From Cincinnati to Virginia we headed.

In the middle of the night, the train stopped somewhere, and we were forced to give up our Pullman beds and sleep in the coach. We were told that no colored person could occupy a Pullman going south to Norfolk, Virginia even if we had Pullman tickets, because Virginia had Jim Crow laws. Some ladies were also in Pullman cars, and they were very upset because they had to change their clothes in the rear of the coach. We had a little make shift restroom. After the train started moving again, we all settled down and made the best of it. Morning came and breakfast was called. We ate behind a black curtain. We arrived in Norfolk late Wednesday afternoon safely, but in poor spirits.

Along with about fifteen more fellows, I was trucked to the U.S. Naval Training Center, Unit B East, in Norfolk. All of us were fed, given our beddings for the night, and assigned a barrack. The next day, I had shots and a haircut; clothing and other Navy things were issued to me; and I was assigned to Unit B and Class eleven.

In Unit B, Class eleven, I met fifty or more new recruits. Boots are what we called each other. Chief Barlow was our drill instructor. Abab, a Filipino, was the steward in charge of us. He trained us in the mess Ward.

During the next few days, I marked my clothing, familiarized myself with other sailors, and I got accustomed to the Navy barracks. I was just one young man among so many other young men. In a week or so we were known by everyone as Class 11, Unit B East, in Norfolk, Virginia. Dorie Miller, the first Black hero in Pearl Harbor, was also in boot camp with me, but he was in Class 10.

All new recruits were restricted to the base for three weeks because we were waiting for results of shots, examinations, and other medical tests. During this period we were given rifles for drill training: mornings and evenings. There were movies and canteens, but no liberty, phone.

I soon learned the Navy Boot song. The song went something like this:

From the farm – from the hills
We gathered here until we created a staunch
*   Navy blue*

Step by step, left and right
We always ready for a fight
As now we are in the old Navy blue
So it's Yo He Ho
You're always on the go
A band of lusty sailors, strong and true
We learn to fight for honor, home and right.
We are proud of the old Navy blue!

We sang that song over and over, every day, every week, every month, along with several other songs that we learned while marching and drilling in a segregated part of the base, of a segregated Navy, and in a segregated city, state, and country!

We, African-Americans, were fenced in on one side, and the white sailors were on the other side without a fence. Every week African-Americans came in and formed classes and they always came to the black side to be trained as mess attendants. All of us black mess attendants, sailors, were restricted to this area. When we wanted to go to a movie or to the canteen, we marched to these places in formation. It was impressed upon us to march and go places in groups. Occasionally, one went alone, but it was very seldom.

A few weeks into boot camp, the Federal Bureau of Investigation, FBI, picked up some fellows out of our unit for escaping prison and other wrong doings. This was quiet disturbing, but we managed to go on. This was life.

Someone Paved the Way

The time arrived when we were finally given shore leaves on Saturday evenings in Norfolk. Occasionally we went up to the Citizen Club to dance with girls, or sat in the Titanic Club for drinks and got drunk; or we went to a movie or church on the black side of town, but more often we just stood on the streets and talked to each other.

All during boot camp in Norfolk, anytime blacks boarded the Navy Base Street Car heading back to the base, a fight broke out between the black sailors and the white sailors. Some white sailor, half drunk, start telling his favorite joke about "Nigger John", the white sailors pronounced it 'nig'gah', and as always some black sailor resented it, and the fight was on. The result: some white sailor got cut up after some black sailor commenced cutting. It was never any time different. It was always started with a "Nigger John" joke, and always ended with some white sailor slashed to ribbons. No one seemed to ever learn from this.

After two months or more of drilling, watching, and learning to serve officers, graduation was forthcoming.

As we neared graduation, I went to a temporary Ward room to learn to set tables, to serve food, to serve trays, and to learn the different kind of cooking utensils, such as round and oblong, and we were schooled on taking orders and serving officers. Abab, our steward, was the person in charge of this training for mess attendants, which lasted two or more weeks.

For graduation, my unit, Class 11, drilled in the open field with music before a few captains and commanders. Several commands were given to us, and we executed them. Then the last command was a passing review; eyes right. We first looked right toward the sitting officers while marching, but we did not look at them directly. Then our drill instructor Chief Barlow commanded us: eyes front, march. We turned our heads front and marched to our barracks in formation.

When we got inside the barracks, we shouted and hollered, "We made it!" We were so glad that we got that far, because some of us did not make it. Most of us thought we would not make it because of the racial tension in Norfolk, Virginia. After we shook hands and congratulated each other, we took off our leggings and threw them away. Throwing away leggings signified that we were no longer in boot training.

After lunch, we turned in our rifles, because we were mess attendants, and we did not need our rifles any more. We felt good that we were Jay Boys in the J-Class. The J-Class meant that we were ready for sea duty on one of the Navy vessel.

After boot camp training and graduation, I was given a fifteen day leave to visit my family and to show my Navy uniform to my friends, and hometown Houston. Even being in your country uniform, racial hatred always raised its ugly head. In railroad and bus stations, eateries, and even restrooms and water fountains, your face, not your uniform, was the first thing people saw. It seems everything and everybody in southern states was against you. Clubs, department stores, movies, and public gatherings were against you.

All of a sudden, you throw up both hands and you were anxious to get back to your unit, buddies, after vacation so you could be shipped out to sea. Hoping and thinking, things will be better at sea. Little, did I know?

Fifteen days were up and I was back in Norfolk, Virginia. I was transferred to the receiving station barracks. Everyday some of my classmates were shipped out which was done in alphabetical order. I waited for my orders to go to sea. While I waited, I had liberty at night. I went to town, along and every so often in groups, everyday until they called me out. I had to be on the base or in the barracks from eight in the morning until four in the afternoon everyday because the yeoman checked on us every single day with orders. But after he came and went, if our names were not on the list to ship out, we could go ashore that evening. I received my orders on December 18, 1939, to go to the USS Arkansas. Little did I know that being at sea was not any different than being on land when it came to racial dissension.

TOUR OF DUTY USS ARKANSAS (Battleship)

Chapter 3

> *"There's nothing either good or bad but thinking makes it so."*
>
> *Shakespeare*

I went aboard the USS Arkansas, called Arkie for short, for duty right after boot camp. The "Arkie" was considered by the crew as a super-dreadnaught that carried about 27,000 tons of displacement. She carried twelve 12-inch guns and also a secondary battery of sixteen 5-inch guns, and anti-aircraft battery of eight 5-inch guns. She got up to twenty knots with her 30,000 horsepower. Her sister ship was the USS Wyoming. These two ships were the first flush deck dreadnaughts of the United States Navy. The USS Arkansas, USS Texas, USS New York were a part of the Atlantic squadron.

After getting squared away in my compartment on the Arkie, I was assigned to several officers' rooms to clean after breakfast each day, tables to serve breakfast, lunch, and dinner, and a battle station.

My battle station was in the ammo hole; and, my duties were to send up powder and shell to the turret guns on the topside. We had only a little training in this area because we were in peace time, but we did practice. Every time general quarters were sounded, all mess attendants ran to their battle stations to send up powder and shells to the topside gun crew. This was not fun. This was extremely hard work.

The gunnery mate was in each hole with a stop watch timing us, and telling us what powder or shell to send up. We used a convey belt to send up the powder and shells. The powder was ninety pound and we had to lift it onto the convey belt and we had to keep it moving. Shells were of different sizes and weights. This was hard and sweaty work too. The gunnery mate timed us and we had to keep the ammo coming. The convey belts were never to be empty.

In a few weeks, I got use to being aboard ship. I wrote letters home and to friends that I was on the USS Arkansas in the "S" division because I was so proud to serve and be aboard the "Arkie", the super dreadnaught.

All the mess attendants, cooks, stewards, storekeepers, ship cooks, bakers, and commissary stewards were in the "S" division. The "S" stood for servant. I got along well with everybody. I slowly caught onto my duties, and learned the best and efficient way to carry them out.

I stood watch in the pantry which consisted of keeping coffee made in the Ward Room. In addition,

Someone Paved the Way

I took coffee up to the Bridge to the officers on watch and every so often to the officers that stood watch on the Quarter Deck – in port. Caution had to be used carrying the coffee because going up to the Bridge, the strong wind would take the tray with cup and saucer out of your hand. But after several trips, I had it covered.

Christmas, 1939, was aboard ship because we were still tied along side the dock. Some officers went on Christmas vacation. Some had duty and they brought families aboard for Christmas dinner. Other officers came and went that day. I got a real taste of serving and waiting on officers because this was a special occasion for them; and, I did not need any static on this special day.

After dinner, I went ashore with some of the other mess attendants. I had lots of fun popping in and out of dances, parties, and other places around town that night.

Everything aboard ship was routine the following week after Christmas. I went out on New Year Eve and brought the year in with friends. I made it in before 8 A.M. because I had breakfast duty, and all of my other regular duties of making bunks, and cleaning on New Year's Day.

New Year's Day, 1940, was about the same as Christmas, 1939. Officers that were on duty had their New Year's dinner aboard ship. Some brought their families for dinner again, and I served and catered to them.

In mid-January, I went to sea. My first experience on the ocean was thrilling, but scary. My first night out to sea was the scariest of all times at sea. I thought, "Any moment now the ship would sink and all of us will die." My imagination ran wild. It was hard taming it that night, because I wondered as to how a large iron ship could float.

I looked out at the sea watching the waves. I would sit out on the deck for hours watching flying fish and sharks swimming and frolicking about. I imagined all kinds of stories about the sea. Some stories would be so scary that I would frighten myself. I would shake with fear. I read a lot about the sea but being there and seeing the real thing was no comparison.

I tried to take the sea all in at once but of course I could not. The sea was breathtaking. I was sea sick the first two or three days at sea; but, as the days wore on, I felt better; and I adjusted to the sea. I overcame my jitters, and really learn to appreciate the calmness of the sea and all that it had to offer. Even when the sea was rough, I felt no fear. After weeks on the ship I stood on the deck and watched the ship roll with the waves in rough water with the serenity of a baby in his or hers mother arms. Being there was one of the best feelings of my life. That was really thrilling.

We pulled into Port Guantanamo Bay, "Gitmo" Cuba, around the end of January. I went ashore and had lots of fun. Monday through Friday, the USS Arkansas, along with the USS New York, the USS Texas, several cruisers, and destroyers were at Gitmo. Some times a carrier took part in battle drills, gunnery practices, and war games. We would go into a port every Friday evening. The USS Arkansas went to Puerto Rico, Ponce, Collabra, and Macaques.

There was lot of racial tension. Southern officers really took advantages of us. They chewed us out because their rooms were not as clean as they thought they should have been, even though, a few were real nasty slobs. We did our best but that was not good enough for some southern officers. Even if we did get the rooms spic-and-span, the southern officers still chewed us out for something.

From time to time we got put on report if the rooms were not cleaned to their liking; more often, there was no pleasing them. We were told off about the way their shoes were shined or not shined. In addition, they were displeased with our serving of food to them. They found something wrong all the time, and they griped all the time, just because they could. We worked steady and hard, but it was no pleasing them.

One of the good things about being on the ship, we were not restricted to any one area, whereas, in boot camp we were restricted. We could go any place on the ship: out on the deck, canteen, to movies, tailor shop, and to the laundry to drop off and pick up for the officers laundry. We could go to any place that the white sailors were allowed to go. There were no separate lines: first comes first served.

One negative thing that we all disliked was being called mess boy on the ship by white sailors and officers.

That was an insult. Seldom did we call ourselves that. Off the ship we were called sailors by them.

Reveille was at 5:30 A.M. for the mess attendants. On some ships it was at 6:00 A.M. A reveille is a signal sounded at about sunrise on a bugle or drum to call sailors to duty.

On the USS Arkansas, my compartment or living quarters was on the 3rd deck as some others. But, my head, toilet, and washroom were on the second deck near the officers' quarters. That arrangement was better for us than the regular arrangement for the white sailors. After washing up, we went to the mess, Ward room to set up tables for breakfast.

After the tables were set up, we went to the officers' rooms to get their shoes for shining. Most of the time, the shoes were just outside the door. However when the shoes weren't there we would open the door quietly and get the shoes without disturbing the officers. We had hell to pay for not getting the shoes or for disturbing the officer. We never made the mistake of waken an officer twice.

Officers were assigned to tables accordingly to rank, and they came in at various times for breakfast, but most often before muster call at 8 A.M. At 8 A.M., the crew and officers went to quarters for muster. All hands fell in by their division for roll call. The mess attendants were exempted from muster. At that time we broke down the tables and had our breakfast.

If any officers missed breakfast because he was late getting up, after muster and calisthenics, the officers came to the pantry for a sandwich or something to eat. At this point and time, his breakfast depended on his previous attitude toward the mess attendants. In other words, if he were a nice and regular toward the mess attendants, the pantry boy would try to find him something, but if he were always giving the boys a rough time and most of the southern officers did, then he had to get the hell out of there. No food for him.

More often than not, those southern officers chewed us out for no apparent reason. They wanted us to break our necks waiting on them. If we kissed up and bowed down to them then we were okay, otherwise, you were put on report or restricted to the ship just for the hell of it; and not giving them breakfast on time or good services was the only way to get them in line or to get even. But most of the southern officers never did learn.

I soon settled down to the fact, that I had six years to do, and that I should make the best of them.

My first major encounter with racial feelings and hatred on the ship were my first time out to sea during a battle drill and gunnery practice. I was assigned to fire watch detail in the officers' quarters while two welders from the ship fitters division welded and repaired a bunk. I stood with a fire extinguisher, prepared to put out a fire if one started. But I had no need to put out a fire while they were welding. After the bunk was repaired and they were finished welding, I went down to my compartment. I made sure they were through and they said they were finished with the welding before I left.

About half hour later I heard the fire alarm. Everyone went to their fire fighting station because that was routine duty. I went also to see if I had to help the firefighters put out the fire. My fire fighting station was not near the fire, so our group just waited until the fire was out wherever it was and everything was secured. It was about 30 minutes later, before I heard Boatswain Mate called "Secure! Secure!" Then we all returned to our respective compartments.

After the fire was put out, the damage control officer inspected the area. The fire and smoke caused a lot of damage to the room, hall, and other parts of the officers' quarters. The captain, executive officer, and the first lieutenant also inspected the area. They found out that a bunk in the officers' quarters had caught fire.

The captain asked questions: What happen and how did the fire start in the quarters' officers? It was explained to the captain about the repair job on the bunk by the two welders. Then the captain demanded to see every man that had a work order or a hand with that job.

First, the master-at-arm took the welders to the captain. The captain asked them how did the fire start. They lied and said, "That mess boy was smoking". Then to the master-at-arm, the captain ordered," Go and get that mess boy and bring him here."

Captain Mass was serious. You went to the brig, jail or you got kicked out after one of the court martial. I

Someone Paved the Way

was in the compartment with the fellows, playing cards, and I was not concerned about the fire or how it got started. It was immaterial to me because the fire was nowhere near my station.

The master-at-arm came into the compartment, and asked Stovall who was on fire watch. Stovall was the head man at that time, better known as the head boy by the Mess caterer who was an officer. Stovall said, "Flenard."

The master-at-arm told me to put on a clean uniform because I was going to see the captain. I did as I was ordered; following him, still not knowing what it was about. On the way there I was thinking: I have been in the Navy less than six months, and I wondered what I have done to draw Captain Mass.

As I approached the bar, there stood the captain, the executive officer, the first lieutenant, the damage control officer, two welders, and their division officer that was representing them.

Division Officer Ashley was there to represent me. As I stood trembling and half scared to death before Captain Mass, the captain looked at my records, giving me time to get myself together. After giving me a little time to get over my fright, he looked up at me and said, "These men say that you were smoking and set a bunk on fire."

Somehow, I mustered the courage and looked him straight in the eyes, and said with trembling lips, "Sir, I don't smoke." He looked at me surprisingly and said, "What?" I replied with a little more courage and strength, "Sir, I don't smoke." He called to my division officer Ensign Ashley and told him to go check this out. "Yes Sir" was his reply.

Ensign Ashley went to the compartment and announced, "Listen up fellows. Does Flenard smoke?" The answer from the fellows in the compartment was, "Flenard does not smoke." "Are you sure?" he demanded. Again their reply was, "Flenard does not smoke."

As I stood before the captain, although still trembling a little, I got enough strength to continue to look him straight in the eyes without feeling so intimidated. Finally, Ensign Ashley arrived upon the Bridge where the Mass was being held. The captain said, "Well?" The reply was, "Sir, Flenard does not smoke."

Silent rang for a long moment before the captain suddenly turned to the two welders and ordered, "Ten days in the brig!" The captain did not say another word but turned and went into his office. Then Ensign Ashley said to me, "Come on. Let's go."

As we were going down the stairs back to the compartment from the Bridge, about three flights down, Ashley turned to me and said, "You are a lucky man." I asked him, "Why am I so lucky? Those fellows lied. They were smoking. They sat that bunk on fire." He turned to me with an angry look on his face and said, "Flenard, you are a lucky man."

He went his way and I went mine; and, as I walked to my compartment, I thought about what he said. My understanding was: if I had smoked, whether I had set that bunk on fire or not, I would have been found guilty, and punished for a crime that I did not commit. But since I did not smoke, I was considered lucky.

After that incident, I had no desire or even try or pretend to smoke, and until this day, I do not smoke. I try to look at that incident in a positive manner: my life was spared for not smoking in all the days of my life.

The USS Arkansas was out to sea on maneuvers when this smoking incident happened. This was around late January or early February 1940.

After three or four more months of gunnery practice, battle drilling, and air raids from the carriers, we headed back to our home port, Norfolk, Virginia.

The ship went into dry dock in Virginia, at the Portsmouth Navy yard for general ship repairs and painting.

Dry dock was an artificial basin to receive ships that have gates to keep the water in or out which is a slip or waterway between two piers to receive ships. Some civilians called the docks wharfs or platforms for loading and unloading of materials.

Dry dock is a dock without the water that can be kept dry for use during the construction or repairing the hull of ships. The ship sat on pillows for easy scraping and painting of the hull. The ship was blown completely dry.

All working parties from each deck division were assigned daily to this working detail except the mess attendants because we were exempted from this cleaning detail. We had rooms to clean and all of our other duties, so it was impossible for us to work that detail.

It was also a messy job. The sailors on this cleaning detail looked like hoodlums after cleaning and scraping all day. They were black and orange from the scraping and painting the ship. They had mask on their noses and glasses over their eyes to keep out the dusk. It was a real messy job.

There was no way we could scrape and paint, then run up to our compartment to clean ourselves up and then serve lunch. So we were glad we were exempted. Occasionally it was a long process, but more often it took only a few weeks for repairs.

During the repair on the USS Arkansas, several officers and mess attendants were transferred, and several new men came aboard. Among the officers being transferred was Captain Pashley. Captain J. L. Hall became the captain of the USS Arkansas. This was in mid-May 1940.

We got weekend liberty: Overnight, 48 hours, and 72 hours leaves. We got overnight liberty without a request but a sailor always had to request 48 or 72 hours liberty. It was never given without a request. Now and then you got it, but more often you did not. Liberty depended on your division officer and his mood, and whether we had problems on board and other unrelated reasons.

The west coast fleet came in during May to the east coast in all seaport cities, such as Norfolk, Philadelphia, New York, on their yearly maneuver. There were a hundred or more ships in Norfolk port with over five thousand sailors on liberty in town every day.

I got a chance to see lots of classmates and friends. Of course the African-Americans were restricted to the black area, Church and Brampton Streets. There were places like the Titanic, and the Citizen Club where all the black sailors gathered.

Mothers, especially black women, were keeping their daughters in doors. Some parents refused to let their children go out because they really hated sailors in this town, especially black sailors. Parents told their daughters not to go down on Church and Brampton Streets, but they came anyway.

I had fun teasing the girls. I also had fun dancing and socializing with the girls that did come; and, I tell you many came and came often. You could not keep some away. They would leave church on Sunday to come and dance with us.

The newspaper headline read "THE FLEET IS IN". That meant good business for everybody. Norfolk was called the Shit City but I never understood why. Go figure.

I enjoyed the fleet in port although, we mess attendants knew there would be a lot of fights between the black and white sailors, with that many sailors in town at one time from different ships in Norfolk on liberty.

We expected a fight each time we boarded the Navy base street car at Brampton and Church Streets. These streets were in the center of the black neighborhood.

The Navy base street car passed through the black neighborhood to get to the base.

Every time a white sailor did something to a black, for instance, white sailors stuck out their feet and try to trip the black sailors as we went to the back of the Navy base street car to sit, or they said something to blacks, and or try to order us on the street car or beach like they did on the ship, a fight broke out with the white sailors being cut or beat up real badly. They usually got the worst end of the deal.

White sailors did not care a bit about black sailors. With that attitude, fights were common. The black sailors that got in fights were transferred. They were called trouble makers.

The last week of May 1940, after leaving dry dock, we made ready for the mid-shipmen cruise. We took on fuel, stores, and other supplies for a two month cruise. We left Norfolk with the Atlantic Squadron that consisted of three battleships: the USS Arkansas, the USS New York, and the USS Texas, two carriers: WASP and HORNET, two or three cruisers and seven or eight destroyers. We arrived in Annapolis, Maryland, in early June, where the Naval Academy is located.

At the Naval Academy, the Cumberland and the USS Reyna Mercedes were docked. On these two ships lived the mess attendants that fed the mid-shipmen at the Naval Academy three times a day.

I saw some of my classmates that were in boot camp with me. They were assigned to the Naval Academy as mess attendants for the mid-shipmen.

The mid-shipmen, future officers, came aboard the USS Arkansas with their own mess attendants. The mid-shipmen slept on the decks in hammocks, but there were more mess attendants than bunks in the mess attendant compartment, so temporary quarters were found for those extra mess attendants on another deck, where blacks usually did not stay.

The mid-shipmen were there for two months for training in all phases of Navy life. It was one big operation: feeding one hundred or more extra men three times a day. The cook prepared extra food and the baker baked extra bread. Topside was crowded, below was crowded, mid-ship and ship company were everywhere on board. Because of the extra people, it was a long two months, even though everything went smoothly. We were one big happy family.

We left Annapolis, Maryland, after five days there. This was my first mid-shipmen cruise. First we went to Guamtanamo Bay, Cuba. After a few days there, we took on fuel and stores. Duties were as usual.

We left Guantanamo Bay and went into the Caribbean Sea to do battle drill and gunnery practice. The mid-shipmen got a real taste of life aboard ship, and all kinds of drills aboard ship. I got a fill of being in the ammo hole. What a feel! After practice, all I could manage was sleep.

After a week of maneuvering, we headed for Ponce, Puerto Rico. There I went ashore and had a swell time relaxing and resting and enjoying the sun, trying to forget the ammo hole.

For two months, every weekend, we were in a different port: St. Thomas, Virgin Island, Kingston, Jamaica, Colon, Panama, La Guiana, Venezuela, Caracas, Venezuela, Port of Spain, Trinidad, and other West Indies ports. This was truly a cruise for all sailors. This was done so the mid-shipmen could relax after a week of battle and gunnery practice. The mid-ship cruise ended after two months of maneuvers at sea.

Near the end of July, after returning the mid-shipmen to Maryland, we returned to Norfolk. The fleet went back to the west coast, and the USS Arkansas took on fuel, stores, and made preparation for the V-7 reserve cruise. The V-7 reserve cruise was for the college ROTC students from all parts of the country.

We arrived in New York City, better known then as The Gay White Way, on the Hudson River in early August 1940.

I went to the World Fair which was very educational. I had a good time. I saw stage shows at the Apollo, and I danced at the Savoy, Small Paradise, and the Cotton Club.

From August to December in 1940, the USS Arkansas made five reserve cruises from New York Hudson River to Guantanamo Bay, Cuba to Colon, Canal Zone, with a total of five hundred young men or more. After days of gunnery and battle drills on each cruise, we returned to New York, for a new crew for Naval training, gunnery drills, and maneuvering, and me in the ammo hole when the quarters sounded. Other times I had regular duties: cleaning, making bunks, and serving the officers assigned to me. All of this became routine to me after a trip or two.

On our returned fourth reserve cruise from Cuba and the Canal, we stopped in Norfolk, for Thanksgiving Day. Some officers went home for the holiday, but others had Thanksgiving dinner on board with their families. I went ashore on liberty after serving dinner to relax and forget some of the harshness from the southern officers that I dealt with every day of the week.

On our fifth and last cruise from the Canal Zone coming into New York outside of Sea Girt, New Jersey, in December, the USS Arkansas had a collision with a freighter. We were not damage, but the freighter was listing and it had to go into some port in New Jersey for repairs. We did not stop to see what the problem was or to help. Instead, we continued on our way to New York to disembarked the reserves.

Christmas Day, we were in Norfolk for Christmas dinner. After serving dinner to my assigned officers, I went ashore to a dance and tried to forget things going on in my head so I would not explode.

January 1941, found me still aboard the Arkie, but not for long. Things were going smoothly. In mid-January, we got under way to Guantanamo, Cuba, again. We arrived in Cuba after several exercises.

WAITING ABOARD THE USS SEATTLE
Chapter 4

"God intended no man to live in this world without working; but it seems to me no less evident that He intends every man to be happy in his work"

Ruskin

"Good news", I was transferred to New York to wait for the USS North Carolina. In mid-January, three of us were transferred to a supply ship coming to Norfolk. There, I boarded a passenger ship to New York. Upon arriving at The Gay White Way, I was transported to the Brooklyn, New York Navy Yard receiving ship USS Seattle.

After settling in and getting squared away on the USS Seattle, I went ashore, toured New York, visiting important parts like the Statue of Liberty and the Empire State Building.

The USS Seattle was my home for two months or more. Other black mess men came aboard within the month. Twenty-five or more stewards, cooks, and mess attendants were boarded, making up a portion of the "S" division attached to the USS North Carolina.

I had plenty shore liberty. I did not have anything to do, just check in and lay around. No duty and no ammo hole for awhile. This was living, but not for long.

The USS North Carolina was dubbed the nickname "Showboat" because she received so much attention during her fitting out and trails. She proved to be the classic battleship functions of World War II. She traveled 27 knots carrying 35,000 tons, smooth as silk, gliding through the water because she had 70,000 horsepower. She carried nine 16-inch guns, twenty 5-inch anti-aircraft guns, sixteen 1.1-inch guns, and twelve .50 cal machine guns.

As the USS North Carolina neared the Commissioned Day, our division officer came aboard the USS Seattle to our compartment with a list of all cooks, stewards, and mess attendants, and our duties.

Ensign Watts said, "Ah-ten-hut! Fall in on the dock!" We listen to roll call before we marched to the USS North Carolina. Our duties aboard the USS North Carolina were to clean officers' rooms, make bunks, put towels in rooms, unpack, wash and store dishes, clean silverware, and clean the Ward room, and anything else the officers asked us to do.

As we pass the mess hall, other mess boys from other ships were eating in the mess hall would raze or hoorah us as we marched onto the USS North Carolina. They would say things like, "There goes the boss taking

Someone Paved the Way

his slaves to the field", and at times "Niggers, to the field." They had a big laugh on us.

Every morning, Monday through Friday, Ensign Watts assembled us on the USS Seattle dock and marched over to the USS North Carolina for a report detail in preparing the officers' rooms, the Ward room, pantry, and officers' Galley.

The weather was rainy in January in New York. We got wet because we did not have rain coats, just our navy peacoats.

We got wet almost every day. One day on the ship, a senior officer came to the Ward room where we were working, asked us how we were doing. We said, "Wet." We asked him to have the shipyard workers to get our compartment ready so we could move in because coming over to the ship from the USS Seattle in the rain, we were wet all day. He said, "That's not good. I will take care of that now and you men can move in today."

After we served the officers, we went to the USS Seattle and moved into our compartment on the USS North Carolina that same day. We were the first crew on the USS North Carolina. We went to the mess hall for our meals and back to work on the USS North Carolina.

The next morning, our division officer Ensign Watts came to the USS Seattle to march us over to the "Carolina". But this time when he went to the compartment, he found two or three mess boys packing, getting ready to move. He left hurryingly, coming to the

"Carolina". We were all in the Ward room waiting for him. He was surprised. He said, "Ah-ten-hut! Messmen Branch fall in for muster." After muster he left. He never said a word to us about moving without getting his permission first. I guessed the officer that told us to move in explained things to him.

Although, we called our division officer Ensign Watts to his face, he was nicknamed Messmen Branch behind his back because he referred to us as Messmen Branch. All the times Ensign Watts came to our compartment, he would say "Messmen Branch do this and Messmen Branch do that". This stuck with us because he pronounced the two words, mess and men as one and us sailors as a branch, so we gave him that nickname. Go figure.

I got my compartment cleaned and squared away. The USS North Carolina was my new home away from home. There were a few officers aboard and other came daily. I was assigned to rooms, tables in the mess room, and watchers in the pantry. Everyone was busy. Messmen Branch made sure of that. He was a cocky little fellow. I learned that he was from some small town in Alabama. So I was always on guard for him for what ever happen.

Everything was falling in place making ready for Commissioning Day. However, the work was hard. The southern officers were plain mean. Messmen Branch was around checking and double checking every room in the officers' quarters, Ward room, pantry, and Galley. Night found us tired and spent, so most of us stayed

Someone Paved the Way

aboard and hit the sack without ado. But some sailors had their wives and girlfriends there in New York, so they went ashore tired or not.

The USS North Carolina was a hot ship. Hot for mess attendants. We were always being sweated and worked long hours. Two or three days before commissioning, Messmen Branch checked and double checked to make sure everything was in order. He appointed one of the mess attendants to be head man, head mess boy. The head mess boy's job was to supervise the mess room duties, cleaning of the rooms, and handling anything concerning the mess attendants.

Other divisions on the ship filled up. Men came daily from boot camps and other receiving stations.

Commissioning Day was scheduled for April 9, 1941. As the ship company made ready for the commissioning ceremony, the mess attendants were not part of the ceremony. Other "S" division groups, such as storekeepers, cooks, bakeries, commissioner stewards were in their assigned place on deck for the ceremony, but not the mess attendants.

April 9, 1941 found us mess attendants rushing from sun up until sun down. We cleaned rooms, set up tables for the visiting officers, before assembling in the Ward room to serve the officers after the ceremony. Admirals and captains from the Navy Department, senators, congressmen, representatives from North Carolina, and others had lunch with the captain in the Ward room. Several Navy officers from the Bureau of Navy had lunch with the captain also. We were dressed in white mess attendant uniforms instead of our regular Navy blues.

So much happened that day. Mess attendants were 'Yes siring' here and 'Yes Siring' there. The only relaxing time was when dinner was over and all the high officials had left the ship.

The watch was set. Duty was performed. The USS North Carolina was a commissioned ship in the United States Navy by five o'clock on April 9, 1941.

TOUR OF DUTY USS NORTH CAROLINA (Battleship)

Chapter 5

"No man is worth his salt who is not ready at all times to risk his body, to risk his well-being, to risk his life, in a great cause"

Theodore Roosevelt

The USS North Carolina was commissioned with a lot of hullabaloo, but the mess attendants did most of the work without ado. We immediately started getting ready for a shakedown cruise scheduled in mid-May.

The mess attendants' duties on the USS North Carolina were the same on other ships. We were to clean officer' rooms, clean all silver, swab and buff the Ward floor, the pantry, the Galley, and to clean the mess room. The same routine duties were on all ships.

Saturday was Captain Inspection Day, and everybody rushed on that day so we could be ready on topside for inspection.

The mess attendants fell in but not with the main "S" division, but beside the "S" division in our own group.

One Saturday, an incident happened after Captain Inspection that further convinced me that duty on the USS North Carolina was hard. Our group passed Captain Inspection, so our Division Officer Messmen Branch called for sock inspection. All men showed their socks. We pulled up our trousers for him to inspect. He said, "What an assortment, white socks, black socks, crap shooting socks, and no socks. All of you are restricted to the ship for the weekend."

Some of the fellows were disappointed because some had girlfriends, wives, and others had plans to go ashore for the weekend. After recovering from inspection, those fellows that were looking to go ashore made themselves at ease in the compartment. The fellows that were on duty in the Ward room set up for noon lunch. Most officers went ashore so lunch and dinner were light.

Another Saturday brought Captain Inspection again. The captain stopped in front of me, looked at me and said, "Sailor, did you shave this morning?" I said, "Sir, I do not shave." He said roughly, "Go down and get that peach fuzz off your face and report back to me." "Yes Sir!" I answered. I went down to the wash room, I washed and dried my face with a towel and came back.

The captain was inspecting another division. I stood at attention waiting. Another officer in the inspecting division party called to the captain's attention that I was back from shaving. The captain walked over and

Someone Paved the Way

looked me over and said, "That's better, fall in with your division." I replied, "Aye Aye Sir."

When I returned to my division standing at ease, Messmen Branch asked me what the captain said to me. I told him the captain said, "Alright Sailor, fall in with your division." That was not exactly what he was asking, but if he wanted to know, then he could ask the captain himself.

After Saturday Captain Inspection was secure and over, the ship began it weekend activities.

Getting accustomed to the ship officers and crew was not easy. Southern officers and crew displayed their banner of hate almost twenty-four-seven. It was not easy to stay afloat with so many southern sailors fighting you, holding you down. In their words, "Keeping you in your place." African-Americans had a place and we were not to venture out. If we dared to be anything other than a servant, we were knocked down. They did not think it was possible for a black person to be a servant and a man at the same time, therefore, it was hard. No it was more than hard, it was hell.

Around mid-May, the USS North Carolina made ready for a shakedown cruise at sea. Everything was tested. Some civilian men working on the ship from the Naval yard were aboard when the word passed over the mike for all hands to report for store detail.

The master-in-arm, police, rounded up all the mess attendants to make sure that we were a part of the store detail. The steward and head boy told the master-in-arm that the mess attendants could not be in the store working party *and* serve lunch in the Ward room at the same time; but, he disregarded it, and, made us pull store duty anyway. We let the cleaning of the rooms go to help with the store detail, which was extremely hard and sweaty labor.

Lunch time rolled around and there was no preparation for lunch in the Ward room for the officers. An officer asked the steward and head boy why the tables were not set up for lunch. The head boy explained what the master-in-arm had done.

The officer was angry. He came out on the deck, and as we came aboard with boxes of stores, he said, "Put that down and go to the Ward room." We did. We washed up, put on our mess jackets, and sat up tables. At half passed twelve, we served lunch.

After lunch, we were told to carry on our regular duties: clean rooms, taking laundry, and etc. The rest of the crew was hot, asking why we were exempted. Hard feelings were shown. A few shuffling, pushing and shoving started. The officer of the deck stepped in, "You men cut that out!" We went about our duties. The executive officer, a commander, heard about the incident. He told the grumbling crew that the mess attendants had their own duties to perform; and, that we were not to go on any more working parties. From that time on, we were exempted.

Taking on stores lasted about three or four days because there were about twelve boxcars to be unloaded. In addition, ammo, fuel, and other supplies had to be loaded.

After all the stores were loaded on board, we made preparations to get underway to sea. The plan of the day or dope sheet let us know that we were getting underway about ten the next day. The next day, with all hands aboard, two tugs came along side and turned us around and within minutes we headed out to sea.

At sea, watchers were set. We went about our duties. Some went top side to wave at passing boats. In a few hours, the shore line began to look like a speck on the horizon. Flanked by two destroyers, one cruiser, the USS North Carolina was gliding along in the sky blue water. On this cruise, all equipments were tested. Guns were fired. Battle stations were practiced. Launching and retrieving planes from our ship and a speed run were tested to check the screws. There was a vibration at a certain speed. The screws needed changing. After about a week at sea, we came back to the Brooklyn Navy Yard and went into dry dock to change the propeller and screws.

The USS North Carolina was in dry dock for a week changing the propellers and other things. After leaving dry dock, the ship moored along the dock for loading fuel, ammo, and stores again.

After cleaning our assigned rooms, during other duties, liberty call was sounded. Those that had early liberty went ashore. Those with liberty after dinner went ashore after dinner. Those with the duty, watched, stayed aboard.

The "Showboat" went to sea to test those things that needed correcting from the first shakedown cruise.

The propeller did not vibrate. There was a smooth glide in the calm blue water. 45 degrees turns practice, right and left, several 90 degrees turns were also practiced. Zigzag courses were practiced also. We returned to port after everything on the "Showboat" was checked.

Things went smoothly for a little while. I settled down to routine duty on the USS North Carolina.

In June 1941, my application for fifteen-day leave was approved.

I went home to visit my family and friends. I had a swell time. All too soon, it was over; and, I had to return to the ax and grind, and to the peculiar habits of the southern officers.

* * *

During the spy round up in New York in July 1941, the FBI discovered we had a spy on board. I left the ship walking towards the Navy yard gate one day, and all of a sudden, the FBI and secret service men closed in on our group of sailors. The FBI shouted, Halt!" to everybody. I quickly froze, so did everyone else. The FBI called out a sailor name. The sailor started to run, but they zeroed in on him, captured him and took him away.

Everybody was buzzing about the capture. Later on I heard from an officer in the Ward room that this sailor had a diagram and list of all ships' name in the Navy yard. Excitement was high on the ship for the next week or two. Everyone was wondering 'who's next'.

Someone Paved the Way

* * *

The months rolled on as the Showboat glided smoothly in the huge expansion of iridescence blue waters that changed colors as we changed directions. But life for the mess attendants did not go smoothly as the ship sailed. Life was hard for us. Southern officers really took advantage of us. They really enjoyed making us jump. They did not let up for a moment. They kept us in our places: servants not humans.

Once I was off the ship, I wore civilian clothes that I kept at the YMCA on Sand Street while we were in New York. Life in the Gay White Way was not so bad. Entertainment was always at the Apollo and Savoy. I had hangouts in the city and Brooklyn where I would go to relax. The months went by slowly and hard.

While in New York I went to the security building for a new identification and picture, which is kept with you at all times.

We were in our home port New York for Thanksgiving, 1941. Dinner was served on ship as usual. Afterward, I went ashore and had a good time at several parties. There was a big dance at the Savoy and Duke Ellington played.

The first week in December, 1941, the Navy yard was calm. Ships lay lazy at the dock, half empty with sailors gone ashore. Sunday, December 7th, I left the Showboat late afternoon, caught the subway train at Sand Street for Manhattan. The subway was coming into 34th Street when someone got on the subway saying that the Japanese had bombed Pearl Harbor.

I got off at 42nd Street, and I heard the news, "All military personnel return to your ship or base." I crossed the platform and caught the next subway back to Brooklyn. The subway was crowded with military personnel. All the Navy personnel got off at Sand Street, and headed for their ships in the Brooklyn Navy yard.

As I walked down Sand Street, people shouted, "War! War! We are at war!" Security was tight at the Navy yard gate, and through out the Navy yard. They inspected everyone. When you were stopped, you showed your pictured ID. I just had received mine a few days earlier. Men returned to their ships in droves, some without their pictured IDs. The yard looked like a mad house.

Aboard, in our compartment, fellows huddled together in groups, talking about the war and what had happened at Pearl Harbor. The next day, Monday, December 8th, the president declared war. A state of war had begun between the United States and the Imperial Japanese government, the German government, and the Italian government. This was World War Two!

All that day we took on stores, fuel, ammo, etc. I knew that we were going to get underway soon because we were under two bridges: the Manhattan and the Brooklyn Bridge. We were afraid of sabotage. If one of the bridges was sabotaged, the USS North Carolina probably would not get out to sea. To prevent this, two days later, we were out to sea.

Someone Paved the Way

The USS North Carolina maneuvered out in the North Atlantic. A few days later, we sneaked back to New York Navy yard, and took on more stores and fuel, and a few more men. This time, we left New York for the last time. We patrolled and escorted a convoy in the North Atlantic.

* * *

Christmas, 1941 and New Year's Day, 1942 were spent at sea.

We came back to the states around the end of January. This time our home port was Casco Bay Portland, Maine. The ship anchored out in Casco Bay. This was about ten miles from the landing where the boats pick up the liberty party. It was very cold and damp, and a bit foggy; but, I enjoyed my new home port.

* * *

Even in war time, the USS North Carolina proved racial problems were much in force. The liberty party assembled on deck on Saturday morning about ten o'clock. The officer of the deck pulled us, mess attendants, out of line. He then let all of the white sailors get into the motor launch first. This motor launch was covered with a canvas top to protect sailors from the mist, sprays, and at times rain.

After the first motor launch was filled, he then called for the second one, which was an open boat to take the mess attendants and a few white guys that did not get on the covered wagon to go ashore. We refused to ride in the open boat because by the time we arrived at the landing, we would be soaking wet from sprays and mist.

The officer wanted to know if we were going ashore. We told him that we were not going to ride in an open boat that we would wait for the covered boat to return. So we went back down below and waited until the covered boat to return. The next liberty party was at two o'clock that day. The covered boat returned and liberty call was sounded. We got in line, after inspection, we were told to get in the boat. The officer of deck stood on deck looking kind of surprise. He did not expect us to go ashore that late in the day.

Later on that night at the USO, we planned to get even. The next morning, we all watched for this dude to come in. "Da da daaa, here he comes!" I said to the fellows. "Ahhh! Good Morning", he said. "What a lovely morning." It all fell on deaf ears. All of a sudden every mess boy was busy, refused to look his way or say hello to him. "Won't someone take my order?" he grumbled. "I have several orders already", one mess boy said. "I'll be back", said another one. While he was fussing because no one took his order, quarters for muster sounded. Some of the officers grabbed a quick bite and a swallow of coffee and out to their division they went.

Immediately we cleaned off the tables, put on the pads, got our breakfast, and were gone by the time muster call was over. After awhile, this dude came to the mess room, seeing everything was cleaned up and no one there to serve him. He went to the pantry looking for a hand out. The pantry boy was swabbing the deck. The dude asked if something was left and the pantry boy said, "We have already served breakfast. We are getting ready for lunch." So he left hungry.

At lunch, the buck where the food began serving was put on the other side of him, making him last to be served. Finally the food reached him. The meats were picked over, potatoes were mushy, and the vegetables were soggy. We noticed redness on his face. He really could not say anything because the mess caterer was a commander, a higher rank than him.

At dinner he was behind the buck again. "What's going on here? I was behind the buck at lunch" he complained. "I don't know, Sir" was the answer he was given. One officer asked him, "What did you do to those fellows?" "Nothing" he said.

After dinner one of the other officers was talking to him. One of the mess attendants told an officer about him pulling us out of the covered boat. We made him suffer another day, but not as much as the first day.

At the ten o'clock liberty call the following Saturday the dude was officer of the deck again. After lining up for inspection, he then called all of the mess attendants by name and told us to get in the covered boat first. We got some real good seats and we did not get wet. Not a mist. No members of the liberty party question this move. Again, at the USO, we planned to take extra special care of this dude.

The following Sunday morning when the dude sat down for breakfast, without asking for service, one fellow gave him a big glass of fresh squeezed orange juice, another one hit him with a tall stack of hot pan cakes, eggs on the side, laced with bacon. Another one hit him with a cup of hot coffee. He didn't have to make a request or wait. We kept the hot coffee coming. We were there for him.

He looked up and said, "What did I do to rate this?" Another officer looked at the head boy and winked his eye. We won that round.

* * *

We were in and out of Portland, Maine on patrol. We got news that three German battleship: the Von Tripitz, Priz Eugen, and one cruiser the Gnersern had slipped through the allied blockade and made their way up to Norway on out into the North Atlantic. Around the last week in March, 1942, we were patrolling up in the North Atlantic and ran upon them. We saw them and they saw us. They got in battle formation, with turrets in the sky, ready to fight, but the USS North Carolina, a cruiser, and several destroyers ran from the fight.

* * *

Back in Portland, anchored in Casco Bay, it was duties as usual. Liberty was daily but nothing exciting. We continued our monthly patrol. We left Portland on the 26th of May heading for Norfolk.

Someone Paved the Way

On Friday, May 28 was lower deck inspection and field day. We cleaned the silver, swabbed and polished the deck in the Ward room. We had everything looking good. We out did ourselves, and we knew we would get top rating for excellent work. The inspecting party came through. The captain saw a dirty coffee cup that an officer left on the side table after sneaking in and drinking a cup of coffee after we had cleaned and left.

I don't know what the captain said but the mess caterer for the officers were very upset. He called all of us to the Ward room. He said that the Ward room was not cleaned properly because a dirty coffee cup was left on one of the tables. He said, "Redo the entire Ward room. Polish the silver again, swab the floor again, do everything again like you have not been here already."

The head boy explained that when we left the Ward room, it was sparkling clean without the dirty coffee cup. The room was clean and ready for inspection. He said an officer must have sneaked in to drink a cup of coffee and left the cup on the table. This information was ignored. He said, "Never mind that, get started cleaning the Ward room over now!" The head boy looked around at all of us for approval and said, "I am speaking for all the mess attendants and we refuse to clean the Ward room again. It is not our fault therefore, we should not be punished."

We stood behind him and we held steadfast.

The mess caterer sent for the master-in-arm, police, and they both tried to force us to work. We told him to do what he wanted to do because we were not going to redo the Ward room. The master-in-arm attempted to shove us around, but we were quick and moved out of his way. One of the mess boys told him, "We will dance a few rounds with you." We got ready for a fast knuckle game but the master-in-arm backed away. He wanted us to turn flips but we did not.

There was a farce between some of the mess boys because some of the guys wanted to go ahead and redo the Ward room to keep peace since the master-in-arm wanted to go to fist city with them, but others refused to let them do anything. Before I could catch my breath two guys started fighting. One said, "You Uncle Tom, SOB, put that mop down!" and snapped him one upper cut. The fight was on, but some mess boys broke it up before anyone was seriously hurt. The mess boy that started the fight went to the brig and later he was kicked out the Navy for instigating a fight.

When the mess caterer saw that we were determined to stand pat and not redo the Ward room, he replied, "Go below. You are restricted."

We won but at a cost of one fellow being kicked out of the Navy. We were restricted to the ship the duration of our stay in Norfolk.

* * *

For the next few days the ship took on stores, fuel, and ammo. Duties were as usual, but the officers did not bother us for a long time. We left Norfolk on June 5th. We anchored in Colon, Panama Canal on the 9th of June.

Someone Paved the Way

The USS North Carolina took on more stores and fuel in Colon. We left for the west coast on June 10th through the Panama Canal. We went through the first lock at 11:30 A.M.; the second lock at 4:00 P.M.; and the third lock at 6:20 P.M. It was an all day thing getting through the Panama Canal but it was exciting.

We rushed through our duties and hurried to topside so we could see the workings of going through the Panama Canal. It was exciting to see. I could reach over and touch the guys working on the Canal. Only one ship could pass at a time. It was something to write home about. And I did.

* * *

June 11th found us on the west coast and by June 30th we anchored in San Pedro Bay. I got a two day liberty pass. I took the Pacific Electric train from San Pedro to Los Angeles. And for awhile I forgot about the ship and the southern officers and their peculiar habits. I had a real nice time touring the city and seeing sights because this was my first trip to California.

* * *

On June 24th, we anchored in San Francisco Bay at 9:30 A.M. We went along side the dock. We took on stores, fuel, and more ammo. We left off all boats and motor launches, in San Francisco. The motor launches were excess weight. We were getting ready for the war zone and the USS North Carolina needed all the space she had for fuel, ammo, and other necessities.

I had plenty liberty for two weeks in San Francisco. I relaxed and had a good time off the ship. In other words, after my duties were performed I could go to the beach or take in a movie or just relax seeing San Francisco.

Certainly I thought about the war zone, but the thought crept into my mind red hot only three times a day: morning, noon, and night.

On July 5th, we left Frisco, entering into the war zone. Saturday, July 11th, we tied up at the dock of Pearl Harbor. As we approached the bay, we saw the results of the December 7th raid. The USS Arizona, the USS Oklahoma, and the USS Utah were sunk, and others were turned over. A few oil spills were here and there. Just seeing this gave me chills and a funny feeling in the pit of my stomach. My thoughts rushed in like an open flood gate. I was sick.

I did not get much relief seeing a two man sub that was captured and on display in the Naval yard. I thought we would have more on display.

After a while, I adjusted to the sights of war and the talk did not bother me as much.

I let my guards down and relaxed a little with the Hawaiian girls while on liberty in Pearl Harbor. They kind of took my mind off the war, destruction, and all that had happened.

We took on more stores, fuel, and ammo. On the 15th of July we left Pearl Harbor to ports unknown.

*   *   *

On July 19, 1942, the USS North Carolina crossed the equator at 1:03 P.M. the latitude was 000000 and the longitude 160'38 w n 153 "53" West.

Friday, July 24th, we anchored that morning in Tongatabu, Tonga Island. We gained a day. Time was set up one day because we crossed the 180 marinas date line. We were in Tonga Island for a short time just to take on fuel and stores. There was no liberty. I did not want any.

We left Tonga Island and did maneuvers and battle drills into the Fiji Islands. Wednesday and Thursday, July 28th and 29th, still found us doing maneuvers, different battle drills which included the mess attendants going to their battle stations in the ammo holes. When General Quarters is sounded, everyone report to their battle station for practice. Occasionally this lasted three or four hours. The ammo hole battle station was a hot and sweaty job. But this was the only action duty that we were allowed. Some of us wished we could go topside and man a gun or something much more worthwhile and or less backbreaking but that was the Navy. You did it the Navy way or no way. Mess attendants had their places and we knew it.

On July 29th, Thursday morning Messmen Branch called all mess attendants, cooks, and stewards to the starboard side quarter deck. He made a short talk. He reminded us that we were fighting for our country and we were expected to do our best. *That entire BS!!* Our battle stations were in the ammo holes. We sent up shells and powders to the topside gun crew. What was so heroic about that?

One of the guys received an article from the Pittsburg Courier newspaper, African-American paper, in the mail. The article said, "African-Americans in the Navy duties were as maids, waiters in the mess room, and in their spare time shoe shine boys. In the time of action their stations were in the ammo holes."

The Navy department heard about this article and the Bureau of Navigation suggested that the Navy reassign some of the mess men topside battle station because of what Dorie Miller had done at Pearl Harbor.

* * *

A few months earlier it was reported to the mess caterer that some of the Filipino and Guamian's boys that were mess attendants did not want to take orders from the head boy which was an African-American. The mess caterer had a meeting in the Ward room with all of us. He told these fellows, "The colored sailors are fighting for their home land also. And if I hear any more about you not cooperating I will make sure that you are on the first ship to Guadalcanal." That kind of stuff soon stopped. They did not want to be on the front line of fire.

* * *

Someone Paved the Way

Monday, August 3, 1942, the USS North Carolina, with a huge task force, went into one of the New Hebrides Islands.

On Friday, August 7, the USS North Carolina along with it huge task force took part in the invasion of Guadalcanal in the Solomon Islands.

For two days things were very hot. There was plenty action. In the ammo hole, I worked my tail off sending powder and shells topside to the gunnery. I did not miss a beat. I kept them supplied. There were no delays or waiting. Boy was it hard and sweaty work especially since the gunnery mate was there shouting orders back to back. "Five inch shell", "Powder!" and etcetera.

I worked steady and hard. It paid off. The USS North Carolina was in control around the Solomon Islands.

Each time I was in the hole, I thought about my life and dying even though the noise from the guns was piercing my ears and I could hardly hear the gunnery mate unless he shouted. I thought, "How will my mother accept my death?" And I wanted to get married and have a family, now I probably will not. All kinds of things went through my mind. At times I was pushed so hard that I did not have the time to think let along the energy. That was good because a person did not need to think about dying while in the hole with everyone on the topside depending on you.

* * *

Sunday, August 9th, we pulled out from the Solomon Islands to refuel. Our main job was to protect the carrier and every now and then escort a troop ship into the bay where they could land more troops.

On Monday, August 24th, while maneuvering in the Coral Sea around 5 P.M., fifty to sixty enemy planes, torpedoes, and bombers attacked the USS North Carolina, and other ships in the task force. Other ship cruisers and destroyers got half of them and the USS Carolina shot down the other half. No bombs or torpedoes reached our ship but one man was killed from a machine gun bullet from an enemy plane, and one sailor was injured during the attack. Everything and everyone else were safe and secure.

The Enterprise, Big "E", was not as lucky. It was hit and set afire. 75 men were killed and 30 men were wounded. The Big "E" was badly damaged as she headed for the nearest port.

* * *

Sunday, September 6th at 12:50 P.M., a Japanese sub launched another torpedo at the USS North Carolina. One of our patrol plane dropped depth charges on the Japanese's torpedo which upset its course and the torpedo went out to sea. It lost it force and dropped to the bottom. Then one of our patrol planes dropped depth charges on the enemy sub and sunk it.

Two weeks later, on Tuesday, September 15th a Japanese submarine pack launched another attack on the US task force and the USS North Carolina was hit this time.

I had just finished serving lunch and all the mess boys were in the compartment. I was over near the portside, standing by the peacoat locker looking at two fellows play some kind of kid game, when suddenly there was this loud boom underneath our compartment. I yelled, "We are hit!" The ship seems to lift out of the water and sway to starboard. I was thrown against some lockers. Fellows standing were thrown to the deck. Those in their bunks were thrown out.

Getting my composure, I ran for the hatch leading up out of the compartment to the second deck. One fellow slipped on the stairs and about five guys ran over him. Upon the second deck, near mid-ship, water pipes were busted. Oil pipes were leaking. There was a terrible oily odor. The ship was dogged down. All the hatches were closed. Lights were out from the torpedo hit. Someone yelled, "Turn on the emergency lights on the bulk head, walls." Someone did and we had some light but not much.

The ship was listed portside, left side. I went around on the starboard side. I was scared, shaking, and praying. For a moment I sat on a ladder leading up to the first deck. I was thinking and wondering what had happened or what was going to happen next. There were about fifteen officers and all of us mess attendants on the second deck trapped.

As I was sitting there contemplating what to do something made me look up? I saw a hatch with a man hole in the center of it for emergency escaping. I yelled, "There's a man hole over here fellows!" Someone yelled, "Where?" I replied loudly, "Over here! On starboard!" I climbed up the ladder to the hatch and began unscrewing the man hole cover. After a few moments I got it open. I went through it into a dark passage. Officers and mess attendants were right behind me climbing out as fast as they could. We held hands feeling our way along the dark passage way. A door opened from the inside. Sunlight was shining in the dark passage way. Suddenly, there was a rush for that lighted door that lead out on deck. As we poured out on deck, looking at the damage, the skipper yelled down on deck, "You men take cover! Take cover!"

I ran for cover.

I was in a sitting position.

I saw the WASP.

The WASP was hit and a destroyer was sunk. Lots of damage were done to our task force. I later learned that the WASP, an aircraft carrier was hit three times. The WASP caught fire and it burn rapidly. Before going down it was listing badly. That sub pack did a lot of damage to our fleet.

We were detached from the fleet after that and we headed out of that area, badly crippled. Five sailors were killed and several were slightly injured on the USS North Carolina.

Several subs tried to finish the USS North Carolina off but she out ran them. We mess attendants did not go down to our compartment for several days. We slept on deck and in the passageways.

Saturday, September 19, 1942, at 11:15A.M., the USS North Carolina badly damaged from Japanese torpedo in the left forward side limped into Tongatabu. Immediately damage control divers went down to access the damage.

Everyone relaxed for a day or two.

That following Sunday, September 20, 1942, I went on liberty in Tongatabu. I bought a couple of souvenirs in town. Then I went upon a hill overlooking the ship. I sat for a couple of hours thinking that we were a long way from Pearl Harbor. I was wondering if I would get back home or not because the same thing could happen to me that happened in the lower compartment. Those five fellows' funerals were today. They were buried on the beach. It was so sad. I could not go. It was more than I could handle.

I went back to the ship later that evening to routine duties.

The damage control team drained the compartments that were full of water from the torpedo hit. While we were in shallow water divers went down again to inspect the damage.

Everyone had funny feelings. The other mess attendants and I talked about the war. We did not want another hit. But we felt it was inevitable. Since we were headed for Pearl Harbor again and the Japanese was determined to stop us from getting there.

On Tuesday, September 22, 1942 at 6:30 A.M. the USS North Carolina left Tongatabu bounded for Pearl Harbor as planned.

* * *

During the invasion on Guadalcanal, patrolling in the Coral Sea, the southern officers had the audacity to use the mess attendants as usual. You would think during war time they would ease up a little. Maybe we could get a break from their constant harassment; but, they were persistence little minded and insecure officers. They took their insecurities out on us.

On our way to Pearl Harbor there was this southern officer that was real mad about something. We assumed the skipper or the commander chewed him out about something he did or should have done. I don't know for sure. That day and as all days, his food was prepared and ready for him on time and the way he liked it. That particular day there was no need for several of us to be in the mess room because so few officers were eating at the time. But he ordered all mess attendants to the Ward room to stand around while he ate. When he finished, he left the table and went to his room without a word to us about dismissal.

The other officers in the Ward room just looked, saying nothing. Finally the head boy told us to go back to our compartment. We were the only ones that he could take his anger and frustration out on. So he got away with it. We dealt with it.

Someone Paved the Way

* * *

Wednesday, September 30, 1942, at 11:00 A.M. as the USS North Carolina came into Pearl Harbor, passing several ships moored at the dock and anchored in the steam or bay, I stood proud to be a sailor serving my country even as a mess attendant and ammo hole loader. I had the best feeling that I will always remember.

As we approached the dock coming from the war zone, all hands on the moored and anchored ships cheered and each and every ship rendered a salute. I stood on deck salty from the sea and tough from battle, accepting the cheers.

The USS North Carolina blew its bugle and saluted back each time a ship saluted. This was the normal procedure for ships to salute each other when they come in from a battle. But it was some excitement for me. Each time we received and sent a salute, I felt chills all over my body.

This I will always remember!

Everybody and his uncle were on the dock waiting for the Showboat. Naval officials, news reporters, and other important officials were there to greet us and assess the damage of the ship.

I sure was glad to be back in Pearl Harbor after two months and 15 days in the war zone. All hands went ashore. I really enjoyed being on solid ground. I had a lot of fun in Honolulu for the next month.

* * *

On Thursday, October 15, 1942, I was transferred from the USS North Carolina in Pearl Harbor to the USS Maryland.

My duty on the USS North Carolina had ended after twenty-two months of service.

The USS North Carolina indeed was a showboat but I was glad to be off her.

War was war! War was hell!

TOUR OF DUTY THE USS MARYLAND (Battleship)

Chapter 6

"It is not what he has nor even what he does, which directly expresses the worth of a man, but what he is"

Henri-Frederic Amiel

The USS Maryland, BB 46, was commissioned April 21, 1921. This was my new home from October 15, 1942 to December 1943. The USS Maryland was 31500 tons big, just a little bigger than the USS Arkansas but smaller than the USS North Carolina.

I had to adjust myself to the ship and familiarize myself with surrounding, areas, and the new fellows. Being in the battleship division, I soon became accustomed to everything.

In addition being a mess attendant, my other duty was still in the ammo hole when we were in the battle mode.

I had plenty liberty in Honolulu for three weeks while the USS Maryland took on stores, fuels, and ammo.

On November 8th we left Pearl Harbor for the South Pacific.

On the 12th of November we crossed the equator. There was always an initiation for sailors going across the equator for the first time. The Shellback whipped the stuffing out of the Pollywogs, first timers. This was not my first time. My first time was on the USS North Carolina. But, because we were in war time, the Shellbacks forego the initiation of the Pollywogs. We did not get whipped or have to do some silly rituals, they just accepted us into the Shellback group. Now that I was a Shellback I had to whip a guy, but he got off easy because I didn't feel like playing games although I was good nature about the initiation anyway.

* * *

November 17, about 7 P.M. we anchored in Levuka Fiji Island in the New Hebrides. Some Fiji people were dark skinned, muscular built, with short black curly hair. They gave us coconuts, bananas, and other island fruits. We gave them gum, cigarettes, ice cream, and cakes. I enjoyed meeting and talking to the native people.

The USS Maryland moored there for two months and a week or two.

We left the Fiji Islands in the middle of February 1943. Two days later we were in another island of the New Hebrides called Havana Harbor Efate. The USS Maryland was assigned to sentinel duty along the southern supply route to Australia and the Pacific fighting fronts. The USS Maryland and the USS Colorado operated out of the Fiji Islands. We patrolled the area for ten months.

* * *

Things went on as usual with duty on the USS Maryland not any different from any of the other ships in which I served. These southern officers were the same as the others and work was extremely difficult because of them. It was the same old stuff but with a different crew.

In the 40's a southern white sailor was a southern white sailor. He could have been on the USS North Carolina or the USS Colorado or the USS Maryland. It was always the same just different names. All of them took out their insecurities out on the mess attendants because we were the only ones that they could mistreat and get away with it. If we said anything, we would have been drummed out of the Navy. I decided that I would not be pushed out of a job because of personalities. So I hung in there, even though it was hard. TOUGH!

* * *

On the USS Maryland my partial compartment was just outside of the pantry and the junior officers mess room. One day I was sitting inside my compartment on a bench while a Guam mess boy named Blas was sitting outside the pantry looking at a magazine that belonged in the mess room. When Blas saw the officer approaching, he quickly threw the magazine down on the floor by the chair, and hurriedly went about his business somewhere else. The officer saw Blas drop the magazine but he did not say anything to him. Instead he came inside my compartment and ordered me to pick up the magazine and put it back in the mess room. "Mess boy, pick up that magazine and put it back in the mess room where it belongs." Although I knew he saw Blas with the magazine, I said, "Sir, I did not have that magazine. Blas was looking at it. He should pick it up and take it in the mess room." The officer became angry and said roughly, "I told you to do it."

He stood waiting to see if I were going to do it. But I moved slowly because I felt I should not have to pick it up and return it to the mess room. He said loudly and roughly, "Hurry up boy!" As I got off the bench slowly, I said softly and mostly to myself, "I am not Superman."

"What did you say, boy?" he asked harshly and surprisingly. I replied quickly and bravely to him, "I said, I am not Superman." He said quickly, "You are on report!" I replied angrily, "OK, I am on report!"

Being on report meant you had to go before the executive officer. The executive officer explained to me that I had disobeyed an order regardless who had the magazine. I should have picked up the magazine and returned it to the mess room as I was ordered. Therefore, I was given ten or twelve hours of extra duty because I refused an order.

I could not explain to the executive officer that I did not refuse an order, but I talked back and that is what the officer got hot under the collar about. It would have gone on deaf ears or worst; I could have been put on report for insubordination because the southern officers did not want blacks saying anything, let along explaining.

When they gave an order regardless if they were wrong or right we had to obey. They felt they were in charge and they could do or say anything to us; and, we should take the guff without a mumbling word.

But there is a limit a person that calls himself a man can take. This was a little incident but it was blown all out of proportion. This officer considered the Guam mess boy more respectable than an African-American mess boy. That was all that was about. Black mess boys were servants and only servants.

My ten or twelve extra hours of duty consisted of shining garbage cans, and mopping decks in some areas of the ship. That meant no liberty.

I did not finish my extra twelve hours of duty because shortly after that I was transferred to the Galley to work as a cook.

I would have had to finish the extra duty anyway but I made a deal with the master-in-arms. I would give him a big ham sandwich or something to eat when he came looking for a hand-out, or if he were hungry between meals for every hour of duty he marked off the sheet for me. He made deals like this with almost all the mess attendants. He always marked us off because he was always hungry or needed a favor or something. That's how I got out of the extra duty. That was one advantage of being a cook. I did not come in contact with that little rebel officer again.

* * *

Shortly after that incident, I got in a fight with some sailors. I went ashore to the island Efate and into the little town and bought several souvenirs one day. I met one of the native girls on her way home. I asked her if I could walk her home. She agreed to let me walk her home. Her home, a hut, was a short distance from the landing where the liberty party was dropped off and picked up to and from our ship.

Most of the native houses and huts were dwellings about the size of a car garage with an opening in front. The floor was dirt with some kind of mat on top of it. There was a cooking place inside the house but with very little other furniture. They slept on mats on the floors.

The girl's home was near the landing where some native men were unloading some huge boxes of cargo.

As we neared the landing on the way to the young lady's hut, six white sailors walked up to me and the one named Red said, "Boy, I want this gal." 'This' sounded like 'disc'. I replied to him, "This town is full of girls. If you want one go into town and get you one." I continued to walk beside the girl. Then Red shot back, "I want this girl." I told him firmly, "Red, I am sorry you can

Someone Paved the Way

not have this girl." I told the young lady to go on home that I would see her later. The young lady said, "OK, I understand." She went on her way. I had the feeling that Red was half drunk and when sailors are half drunk, mess always starts.

As I stood there facing these six white sailors that were not drunk but I could tell they had a few beers. They had just enough beers in them for courage to act stupid. Red was from the fourth division which was next to the Galley where I worked. So we knew each other. Everyone at the landing was looking at us. There was a quietness and stillness about the place that gave me the courage that I needed. None of us moved nor did the working crew. They were silent and still. Everyone seems to just freeze, including me, waiting for someone to make the first move.

Red and his five friends really did not want the girl. They wanted to pick a fight with me. I was *ready*. But I waited for them to make the first move and Red did.

I ducked as Red swung and missed. Then I swung and struck him with a sever blow to the left eye and nasal area. He fell back and bellow out, "That nigger hit me." As Red was getting up off the ground wiping blood, another little white sailor named Nazzero, who came to my compartment to listen to my latest records, was battling head down with one of the five remaining fellows in front of me. I don't know from where he materialized. But he was there going one on one with one of the half drunk sailors. The other four were watching and whooping it up and urging the fight on. "Get 'em Red!" "Sock the nigger where it hurts!"

Before Red could recover completely from the shock of being hit, I got my knife out of my pocket which was a push switch blade that I bought in New York.

Red got off the ground and started toward me swinging and missing. Seeing the knife in my right hand he stopped suddenly. I was talking trash to him. I sung a song, "My name is knife. I live on Cutter Street, next to the Butcher Shop. If you don't believe I know how to use this thing, come on!"

All six of them froze again. They stood looking at me. I know they were wondering if they could take the knife without one or more of them getting seriously cut. It took them some time to think. In the meantime, Nazzero, the little fellow that was helping me out that was from Rochester, New York, hollered to me, "Hey Flenard, don't cut me. I am on your side." I said, "OK, I see you Nazzero."

Before Red and his friends could think of what to do next, Middlestaff, who was in my division, said to me, "I'll take that knife Flenard." I said to him, "The doctor said take medicine, not my knife." He shot back, "Boy, I am from Mississippi and I would love to put this stick on your head!" I responded, "If you hit me Middlestaff, I will kill you. If you think I am lying, hit me!"

Out of the corner of my eye, I noticed the shore patrol officer watching. He turned his back and walked away. As I stood there waiting for them to charge into me, two things came to mind.

One incident just happened a week earlier with another mess boy named Riley from our ship that went ashore on liberty. Somehow he got into a fight. Six or more half drunk white sailors beat the living daylight out of him. They broke his nose, closed both eyes, and broke some ribs. He was beat so badly, he had to go to the sick bay on the ship. Later they transferred him to the base hospital in Pearl Harbor. They claimed that Riley started the fight by calling the white sailors names. Nothing was done in the way of punishing those fellows for nearly killing Riley. I made up my mind that sort of thing was not going to happen to me.

The second thought was from an old black fireman from the Navy that I met some time ago heading back to the ship from Norfolk on the Navy base street car. I sat beside him and struck up a conversation with him. He was a fireman in the Navy when they used coal burner during World War One. So he was allowed to keep his rank as fireman. We talked about different things before he said, "I am going to give you a piece of advice." I listened as he spoke. He said, "Buy you a knife and let that be your shipmate. Take it with you where ever you go because there will come a time when you will need it. It may not be any other fellow, black mess men, around you can depend on. Your shipmate will help you out in a many scrapes." He continued, "When half-drunk white sailors pick a fight with you, and you are alone, and with nothing to protect yourself, they will beat you to death. But if you have your shipmate that makes the difference."

When we reached the Navy base, the old fireman went to his barrack and I went onto the ship.

I heeded his advice. I got me a shipmate.

Suddenly a hand touched my left shoulder forcing my attention to the problem at hand. I looked around. There stood one of the natives to the left of me. He said, "Me see you fight." Casually I glanced at him and said, "Yes I am fighting these fellows." He asked, "You fight like Joe Louis?"

After discovering what he was saying about Joe Louis, quickly I said, "Joe Louis is my brother." This time he came closer to me and asked, "Joe Louis is your brother?" I said, "Yes, he is my brother and if you want to help me, go and get two or three more fellows."

He hurried away hollering something in his native language to some other native men. Within seconds four or five six footers, muscular built dark skinned, with black curly hair fellows were standing on both sides of me. He had told them that Joe Louis was my brother and they came to help me fight.

The natives greeted me jovially but with a lot of respect. "Hi de Joe Louis's brother." And "Glad to meet you." They shook my left hand because I was still poised with the switch blade in my right hand ready to cut some butt if push came to shove.

I looked to the right of me, Nazzero was standing beside one of the big fellows with his fists up and poised in a fighting position ready to do battle. Nazzero was white but he was okay in my book. I smiled to myself. I asked one of the fellows, "Are you ready to help Joe

Louis's brother fight?" One said something in his native language to the others and there were loud grunts, indicating that they were ready and we stepped forward. The natives had their dukes up in a fighting position, and I had my shipmate up and back ready for sticking and cutting.

Seeing the heavy artillery advancing, the oppositions turned yellow as their courage slipped down their legs. They backed off. We paused for a few minutes. We moved back to the boxes, laughing and talking. I showed the big fellows a little shadow boxing, and how Joe Louis would knock out his opponent.

The shore patrol officer and Middlestaff moved near the boat landing to wait for the boat. The boat came in shortly after the skirmish. A call for all men going to the ship was sounded.

One of the native fellows walked with me and Nazzero down to the boat. He stood on the dock as we got into the boat. No one said a word, just stared at me. Nazzero and I sat on the starboard side. I still had my knife open, still in my hand.

A white sailor sat on the other side of me, he didn't see the ruckus, but he sensed there must have been some trouble because the others were staring at me in a threatening manner, and I sat with an open knife.

I looked at the fellow sitting by me with a non-threatening look because I knew he felt very uneasy sitting beside me with an open knife.

As the boat pulled out, the shore patrol officer stood on the landing looking down at me in the boat. Still no one said anything. Not a peep from Red or his gang.

The loading boat soon reached the ship. As I went up the gang way, from inside the boat, I closed my knife and slipped it into my pocket.

I saluted the flag and the officer on deck then I went down to my compartment.

I told my buddies what happened. They called them some choice names and said that I should have killed all of the SOB's, but I knew better. I only wanted to save myself.

* * *

Things seem to have quieted down when we left Efate, New Hebrides on the second of August. We joined and maneuvered with the task force. We pulled into Esparto, Santo, on the 5th.

We took on fuel and left for Pearl Harbor on September 7th. We arrived two days later. While in Pearl Harbor we installed additional 40 mm anti-aircraft for more air protections due to the heated campaign in the South Pacific for the first time in ten months.

I went ashore to a movie and later to a dance trying to get the war off my mind so I could come back to the ship and do an excellent job in the ammo hole or where ever I was needed. It worked. I relaxed. I forgot. I had fun!

* * *

A month later, we headed back to the Southwest Pacific to Efate, New Hebrides. The crew sensed that something big was about to happen and we were going to be in it. There were too many ships forming in the area. A vast amphibious campaign was in progress. The USS Maryland and her sister ships played a key role.

We left Efate late one evening. We were several days at sea before several ships in this southern attack force all showed up.

Around late October, we started shelling at 4 A.M. in the morning at Tarawa in the Gilbert Islands.

For five days we bombarded them, fought off fighter planes, and called fire assignments in support of one of the most gallant amphibian assaults in history.

I worked my tail off in the hot ammo hole. But as usually I kept the shells and powder moving. We secured the island. We finally had complete control of Tarawa after a week.

I learned later, fighting was hard and tough for the US marines on the island and many were killed.

For a week after the island was captured, we remained in the area protecting transports and ships that brought fresh troops to the island.

* * *

We returned to Pearl Harbor again. We were transporting two captured Japanese prisoners to Pearl

Harbor when the battery store room caught fire and exploded. That area of the ship was damaged badly. Causes were never determined.

Security officers in Pearl Harbor relieved us of the prisoners.

I had liberty for a day.

We took on fuel, stores, and the mail. We left the next day bound for the states.

We arrived in San Francisco a few days before Christmas. I enjoyed Christmas in San Francisco.

I was out of the states for 18 months. It was good being back in the states.

* * *

Good news: I was being transferred to the USS Bountiful which was under construction in San Francisco. Commission Day was scheduled for late March or early April 1944.

I was given a 30 day leave. I went home to Houston to visit my family. I saw a lot of friends. I relaxed and talked about a lot of things that were not war related. I visited the family church, having a good time worshipping and giving thanks to God for sparing my life so far.

TOUR OF DUTY ON THE USS BOUNTIFUL – AH 9

Chapter 7

"Any heart turned God-ward, feels more joy in one short hour of prayer, than ever was raised by all the feasts on earth since its foundation."

Bailey

I returned to San Francisco to ship out on the USS Bountiful in February 1944 after a 30 day visit with my family and friends in Houston.

I was stationed at the receiving station on Treasure Island where the rest of the crew for the USS Bountiful was being quartered. We were there for three months waiting for the ship to be commissioned.

The USS Bountiful was a hospital ship that was converted from the USS Henderson transport. Everything was rebuilt except the engine room and the navigating equipments.

I went aboard about two weeks before Commissioning Day which was on March 23, 1944. On Commissioning Day the mess attendants stood with the "S" division on deck.

The USS Bountiful had two separate crews. One crew was to sail her and under the watch-ship of Commander George L. Burns. Burns was from Massachusetts and his line crew consisted of 150 men. Of these 150 men, 35 or more were mess attendants. Two cooks and two Galley fellows worked in the officers' Galley. I was one of the officers' cooks.

The other crew was the medical staff under the command of Captain Roy Fulton of Washington. The medical crew consists of 15 medical officers, three dental officers, three hospital corps officers, 21 Navy nurses, and 150 hospital corpsmen. The medical staff took care of the sick and wounded until they were transferred to a hospital ashore.

The two commanders seem to have no problem handling things together as a team.

The USS Bountiful carried no more than 500 patients at a time; although, she was the equivalent of a 700 bed hospital ashore. She had all the equipment that hospital of similar sizes ashore would need, as well as, a lot of special gear for her own particular purposes.

On April 1st, we left San Francisco for Honolulu with 500 women and children that we were transporting back home. This load of passengers left Honolulu during the Pearl Harbor emergency. We stayed long enough to get service then we return to San Francisco with 500 or more hospital patients scheduled for the Veteran Administration Hospital and other hospitals.

Later on, we returned to Honolulu with another group of Navy wives, families and children.

On May 1st, we left Honolulu, sailing toward the Western Pacific and we arrived off the Saipan invasion beaches in June. The USS Bountiful was filled with 500 or more casualties from the Saipan invasion. In an hour or two we headed for Honolulu again. We transferred the wounded marines to the hospital in Honolulu.

The USS Bountiful made three passages to the hospitals on Kwajalem in the Marshall Islands with casualties of the Marianas invasions and back to Honolulu while the American forces continued their victories sweep across the Pacific.

* * *

The USS Bountiful had a restricted area known as "Nurse Country". The crew was not allowed except this did not apply to mess attendants, stewards, and cooks that worked in the nurses' quarters. With women aboard and mess attendants in their rooms and quarters, most of the crew had a dislike for the mess attendants.

One time, I was talking to a head nurse, one of the crew stopped to hear the conversation. The nurse turned around and asked, "Yes, can I help you?" The sailor replied, "No." Then she said, "Well go about your duties. This does not concern you." I got the meanest look a sailor can give to another sailor without doing some serious damage. But that did not bother me.

There were hard feelings between the crew and the mess attendants because the crew did not like the idea that the mess attendants were allowed in the nurses' quarters, of course for cleaning only. The tension was so thick that you could cut it with a knife.

Insulting and degrading words were passed back and forth but no one passed a lick because fighting on the ship was strictly forbidden. You would get kicked off the ship and maybe out of the Navy.

* * *

I got liberty any time I wanted it because I was a cook. I took to the island like a duck takes to water. I was glad to get off the USS Bountiful due to the tension of blacks against whites because of the white females on board.

I spent seven months on the USS Bountiful cooking for the officers while the first crew manned the ship and the second crew took care of the wounded.

I was transferred to the USS Argonne as a cook for the Flag in early September 1944.

TOUR OF DUTY THE USS ARGONNE (Submarine Tender)

Chapter 8

"We are all of us failures - at least all the best of us are. The man who is in real danger is the man who thinks he is perfectly safe."

Sir James Barrie

The USS Argonne was a naval transport service ship converted to a submarine tender. She operated along the Pacific Coast as Flagship and Tender of Submarine Division 20. She flew the flags of Commander Bare Force United States Fleet.

While operating with the fleet in the Pacific, the USS Argonne was at Pearl Harbor on December 7, 1941, but she escaped the bombing without damage. She assisted in repairs of naval vessels at Pearl Harbor. She also served the fleet with repairs and savage operation at the following locations: Narimeu, New Caledonia, New Zealand, Espiritu Santo, New Hebrides, Marshall Islands, Manus Islands, and others.

I came aboard the USS Argonne in Manus early September, 1944. I was the cook for the Commander Train Fleet Bare Force, Flag. I really did not have time to get to know the fellows, mess attendants, because my stay was so short on the USS Argonne. I refused to cook some smelly meat. For that, the mess caterer accused me of not working with the steward. So they decided the best thing for me was to be transferred to another ship.

I lost my chance of a promotion because of this.

My stay was from September to November 1944, which was two months or less. I probably made history being on a ship for only two months.

* * *

While waiting for my replacement, on November 10th, anchored at Seeadlen Harbor, the Mount Hood AE11, an ammunition ship was berth adjacent to the USS Argonne. The ammunition ship exploded.

I was cleaning the range in the Galley when I heard a loud boom. Before the loud noise, pots and pans began falling in the Galley. The range top slid on the floor and several things over turned on the floor. The loud boom sounded. Several fellows fell to the deck.

My first reaction was to get out of the Galley. I ran out into the passageway that leads out on the deck. Everyone on the deck was running inside and yelling, "Go back! Go back!"

They were telling us to go back because pieces of steel, red hot like fire, were raining down on all the ships and boats in the harbor.

I turned around and ran to the other end of the deck to an anchor shelter in the bow. An officer was in front of me. As we neared this shelter a large piece of hot steel from the exploded ship flew toward us with a buzzing sound. It landed behind us. It missed us about a foot. Before we reached the anchor shelter, another piece of hot steel, about the side of a chair, slammed into the top of the anchor shelter right in front of us.

I turned and ran back to the mid port of the ship for cover. A few minutes later, when the explosion had ceased, I came back out on deck to check out things. The harbor was black with smoke and little pieces of steel about the size of small eggs were still flying in the air, hitting the ship. One piece of steel hit the bulkhead just over my head. I dropped down on one knee and duck-walked back inside.

Moments later, I ventured out again and looked around. Things were sort of quiet as the smoke began to rise above the water and dissipate. Steel pieces were still falling from the sky landing on our ship with deadly thumps.

There was a huge clean space where the mounted hood was anchored. It was gone due to the explosion. All the small crafts, boats, ships in the vicinity were sunk except the USS Argonne. But some of the USS Argonne crew was lying out dead on the deck. Some men were killed in sunken boats and others by flying hot scraps that must have flew 5 to 10 miles per hour.

Other members of the USS Argonne crew ventured out after the noise and they were equally shocked as I was.

The officer of the deck said, "You men give me a hand here." About three or four of us went down to the gang plank in a motor launch where several men were killed from flying steel. Stretchers from the sick bay were handed to us and we put the dead men on the stretchers and brought them upon the deck. One of the dead men had turned blue. I wondered why.

After awhile I went back to the Galley and started cleaning up the debris there. Shortly, the other cooks came in and helped with the cleaning. It was a real mess. We worked steadily for awhile with no one talking because it was such a shock. We had to get our bearings and reformulate our thoughts before talking. Finally a cook said, "What happened?" and we all started talking at the same time, asking questions that we had no answers but a whole lot of speculations.

I thought the Japanese had had a bombing attack raid on us in the harbor. It was an hour or so later someone stuck his head in the Galley's door to let us know that the ammunition ship blew up.

All that day, men on boats were in the water picking up bodies. The explosion happened so fast that no one knew exactly what caused the explosion and why all of those men got killed. We mess attendants suspected friendly fire.

I could not help but think, "Am I next? Will something like that happen to me?" I knew accidents happened and yet it is hard to adjust to or understand when something like that happens. I had to pray to keep my mind on work. Everyone on the ship was quiet. But I knew they were thinking just like me. Why would they allow an ammo ship to anchor in the middle of the harbor? Ammo ships always anchor way out. Some senior officer present afloat, SOPA, will have to answer some hard questions. I knew some heads would fly also.

The USS Argonne suffered several causalities and much damage from the explosion.

No one found out why the ship exploded and why so many had to die before I left the USS Argonne.

My replacement came in a day or two after the explosion. This was mid-November. I was transferred to the USS Endymion.

The USS Endymion came to Manus on her way to Kossal Passage. She had missed the explosion.

While on the USS Endymion, I heard the USS Argonne had another freak accident. She suffered serious damage but no one was hurt when a depth charge was accidentally set off by the impact when a small craft bumped into the sub-charger which was moored along side the USS Argonne.

I was glad to leave the USS Argonne.

TOUR OF DUTY THE USS ENDYMION (ARL 9)
Chapter 9

"Labor, the symbol of man's punishment;
Labor, the secret of man's happiness.

James Montgomery

The USS Endymion was commissioned May 9, 1944. Lieutenant A. Edgell was in command. This ship was converted from L.S.T. and reclassified to ARL 9. She was 1625 tons empty and 2220 tons loaded. Her speed was not too fast, only eleven knots but she served her purpose, which was to make repairs on ships and from time to time escort convoys through the South Pacific.

After being commissioned and on a shake down cruise in the Chesapeake Bay, she sailed for Guantanamo Bay in Cuba guiding a convoy to Panama to San Diego continuing onto Pearl Harbor then to Guadalcanal.

Lieutenant Edgell had a 200 men crew and twenty-two of those were mess men. The crew consisted of naval reservist, 90 days wonders, with the exception of two regular Navy officers promoted from the deck.

In mid-November 1944, I was assigned to the USS Endymion in Manus as a regular US Naval officer's cook. We left Manus Island through the Kossal Passage and joined a convoy of ships heading for Leyte Gulf in the Philippine Islands.

Before we arrived in the Philippine Islands the US Navy fought the Japanese Navy and they won that battle hands down. We stayed in the Philippine Islands a month or more. The USS Endymion's duty was to repair damaged landing crafts.

* * *

My cooking duties were routine. Getting adjusted to the guys, mess attendants, and their constant griping was a problem.

They griped that the duty stunk. They griped that the officers were mean. They griped that the food was bad. And they even griped that the weather was bad. They griped day and night.

The truth of the matter was they did not want to be there. Therefore there was no pleasing them. It was only twenty two of us, why couldn't we keep it together?

Finally I stopped socializing with them. I kept to myself. The negatives were more than I could deal with. I knew there were a lot of problems but I learn early on in the Navy to deal with them in a manly fashion.

Griping has never made things better for the African-Americans. So why complain?

* * *

While we were anchored in Leyte Gulf several boat loads of Philippine natives came out to our ship begging for food. Some of the natives were naked and others had only fragments of clothing. The Japanese left the Philippine Islands stripped.

After being defeated the Japanese that survived took everything with them. I didn't understand how the United States could have let that happened. If it were left up to me, and if the Japanese were allowed to leave, they would have left empty-handed. They should have been thankful for their lives. They had no need to take all the clothing, furniture, and food.

Every morning and evening I would give the boat people food that was left over from breakfast and dinner. And there were lots of food left over. Now and again we made stacks and stacks of pan cakes, ham, and bacons and the officers would not eat a morsel of it. We had cooked a lot of food so in case the officers wanted it, they would not have to wait for it. They were quiet mean if they had to wait. So food would already be prepared for them. We never knew what they wanted to eat. So we prepared a variety of foods, just in case.

Whatever was left I would put in a large tin can and lower it down to the boat people.

One day I was handing out food to the boat people, an officer ordered me not to give them any more food. "Throw it over the side", he said.

I sure hated to throw the food in the water but that was an order. Even with the food being thrown in the water, the boat people grabbed it up out of the water and ate it. It was hard for me to watch them grab wet and soggy food out of the water and eat it.

I really felt sorry for these people. So whenever the officer was not around I disobeyed orders. I put the food in a can and lowered it down to them anyway. But I made sure the officers were no where around, but if they were I threw the food into the water as ordered. What an order? Go figure.

I was invited over to visit some of the families in their huts. I made quite a few friends. The women with children came first with me. I made sure that they got the cans of food first. I even threw out old Navy clothing and discards for them to wear. They were grateful to me but I knew not to feel pleased that I was in a position to help them. It could have been me. Worst had happened to my forefathers. Slavery!

* * *

It was reported that a few snipers were hidden out on the islands. Even though we searched for them going ashore was a bit risky.

One day, I was on my way to the Recreation Field. As I neared the wooded area, a sniper came out from his hiding place to eat food from the garbage can. We saw each other at the same time and we scared each other. We jumped and then we both ran in opposite directions. He ran one way and I ran another way.

Then I realized that he was the enemy. I stopped and yelled, "Hey you! Stop!" but words fell on the ground. He was out of sight before I could catch my breath.

I told the fellows at the Recreation Field. I said jokily, "The last time I saw him he was making it." We had a good laugh, but we were kind of scared after that. We were more watchful after that.

* * *

Christmas, 1944 and New Year, 1945 found me still on the USS Endymion at Leyte Gulf, Philippine Islands.

Since I was the cook in the Galley, I did not come in contact with any of the officers often. Several times, the mess caterer stopped by the Galley and talked with me about regular Navy and the ship. He also told me if I got into any trouble I could always come to him.

I am sure he knew why I was transferred to the USS Endymion. I think maybe he appreciated the fact that I refused to cook and serve smelly meat to the officers. He was not a southern officer but he was trying to butter me up to reenlist when my time came to go out. He found nothing more satisfying than being in the Navy, traveling around, seeing new sights, and meeting new people. I sort of liked him anyway. I never had a need to go to him, and if I did, I probably would have not gone to him. I was my own man. I handled my own business and problems.

* * *

For the next two months, we continued repairing damaged ships so they could return to Pearl Harbor. In mid-February, we joined a task unit for the invasion of Okinawa. The task force consisted of battleships, carriers, heavy and light cruisers, destroyers, mine sweepers, and troop ships. This was one great armada of ships. It took over a month before all the ships were united together to leave for Okinawa.

* * *

On April 1st Navy's battleships began firing at shore batteries and guns of the Japanese. Along the coast, planes from the carriers dropped tons of bombs on shore. Fighter planes fought off Japanese attack from Tokyo and the Manchurian areas.

All mess attendants were at our battle stations all day. My battle station was on one of the 20mm guns. I was second loader, and it was hot and sweaty work. The anti-aircraft guns from the larger ships kept the Japanese fighters and bombers away.

Japanese's Kamikaze plane attacked the US ships in the harbor. One US carrier, the USS Bunker Hill, got hit and was damaged very badly by Kamikaze planes.

A Kamikaze plane carried a pilot and a 500 pound bomb with the sole purpose to commit suicide by crashing the plane and bomb on a US ship.

This was very affected around Okinawa. Those Japanese guys did not mind dying. It seems that was their sole purpose in life: die trying to get the US ship. Many died trying. Some succeeded.

* * *

The USS Endymion was in the Naha Bay for sixty-seven days, from April 1st until June 7th.

There were times the USS Endymion was the only ship in the harbor. Every single day we made smoke from our smoke foggers to conceal and protect our ship from the Kamikaze planes. The smoke would hide our ship from the Kamikaze planes. The pilots had to almost land to find us. If they did get close to the land they usually crashed and burned before they could spot us in the smoke and fog.

Most of the times, we shot them down when we heard the planes near by before they could spot us. Every now and then they crashed and burned far away from us thinking maybe they would get lucky.

We did, however, repair damaged ships that were hit while out on patrol or on the picket land so they could return to Pearl Harbor.

On April 28th the USS Endymion suffered damage from shrapnel burst. Several members of our crew were injured from friendly fire.

On May 10th we moved over to Buckner Bay from Naha Bay where we underwent daily attacks from suicidal planes, although our repair service to damaged ships was never interrupted.

* * *

One incident happened and I felt sorry for the fellows aboard the troop ship anchored not far from us on the port side. They were kidding and razzing us about how they were going to win the war. We just looked at them because our ship was a repair ship. Although we defended ourselves, we did not go out to fight as other ships did.

Later that evening general quarters were sounded, "All hands man your guns." I ran to my ammo hole and I was ready. There was an attack. Most of the Kamikaze planes were shot down but a Kamikaze plane dove through all of the anti-aircraft fire and dropped on the anchored troop ship. Bomb and plane exploded. Several soldiers were killed instantly. Several fires started and lots of soldiers that were ready for disembarking jumped over the side and many of them drowned.

I felt real sad for those fellows because there was nothing any one could do to put out the fires. The soldiers had little choice: wait to be burned to death or jump aboard in deep and choppy water. By the time we knew the air was clear and we were free of danger, everything and everybody was in a confused state.

Some sailors threw several life savers out and lowered dinghies, some soldiers were rescued but too many drowned.

Someone Paved the Way

It could have been the USS Endymion that was bomb. It could have been me in the deep and choppy water.

Air raids were frequent. In the morning, high noon, and in the evening, the Kamikaze planes kept coming. It seems as if there were a million suicidal Japanese. They all had death wishes, however many it was.

* * *

Everybody was on edge. Nearing the last of May 1945 our captain could not take it any longer. He said, "Let's go home."

On June 7th we left Buckner Bay for Pearl Harbor through the enemy zone instead of going the long and normal route to Pearl Harbor.

The captain was stopped by the executive officer but not before we were smack in the middle of the war zone. The captain was confined to his room until we reached Pearl Harbor.

On June 21st, about 7:30 A.M., the USS Endymion was torpedoed. The fantail, rear, seem to raise-up in the air, sending pots and pans in the Galley crashing to the floor. Several fellows slipped and fell backward on the Galley floor. The food went flying through the air before landing on the floor. Everything went topsy-turvy. In moments, everything was in totally disorder.

I picked myself up and ran out on deck on the starboard side to see what was happening. I looked out over the water, and rising up out of the water was a

Japanese submarine. Several men were emerging from the sub hatch and running toward their guns. I knew that they were going to open fire on us and finish us off.

I ran through the passageway to the port side for cover. I lay down on the deck near the angle iron, waiting for the first shots from their sub five inch guns. As I laid there thinking how much time it would be before they started shelling us, I heard a droning sound in the sky and I looked up.

I saw a silver object. It looked like a plane flying low in our direction. The Japanese men on the submarine looked up and saw the plane too. I knew I was not in a safe place.

As I got to my feet, I saw the Japanese cover their guns and run for the hatch. As I ran back through the passageway to the starboard side I saw the submarine submerge beneath the surface of the water.

Momentarily I froze in my tracks. I did not understand what was going on. I thought for a second that the Japanese submarine had no need to fire on us because their plane would take us out. Then I thought, they should have stayed up and helped their plane to finish us off. I did not understand their strategy. So I ran for cover and waited.

I never heard any firing. As I waited I heard the crew talking about the submarine and the plane that kept going. I came out of hiding to get the whole story. The crew was discussing the plane. It could not have been ours because if so it would have fired on the sub.

Someone Paved the Way

And if it was their, they would have fired on us. The plane did neither.

Finally, the navigator and the executive officer and several other officers went down into the after steering room to check the damage. They discovered that the rudder was bent, the steering column busted, and the only way we could steer the ship was to do it manually, by hand.

The radar system was completely knocked out. No communication could be sent out or received. The USS Endymion was in a bad way.

I wondered if we would make it home.

The executive officer was Johnny on the Spot. He quickly set phones up from the Bridge to the after steering room so we could communicate to each others on the ship, but outsiders could not receive our messages and locate us.

The executive officer put the USS Endymion on a zigzag course for safety: two degrees right and two degrees left, then four degrees right and four degrees left, then two degrees right and three or four left and back and forth. The ship was going as fast as she could: about six knots, trying to get away from the Japanese submarine.

I learned later that the torpedo exploded when the rear of the ship was up on its roll. Otherwise the torpedo would have hit us smack in the middle and sunk us for sure.

In fear of the plane that flew over, the submarine remained on the bottom of the sea giving us a chance to get away. All day, we watched for the Japanese sub's periscope.

Later that evening we saw a fog bank coming toward us. The acting skipper said that if we could get to that fog bank, it would be impossible for that submarine to see us.

That night, we were in the fog. It was so thick you could not see two feet in front of you. The acting skipper gave a short talk. He warned us that the submarine was hunting us to finish us off, and we had to be quiet, extremely quiet.

"No loud talking because your voices carry on the water", he told us.

We had a dog on board as our mascot. He was put below deck in one of the store room so if he barked, he could not be heard.

About two hours in the fog, we heard the Japanese fellows talking. They had caught up with us but they did not know it because of the thick fog. They were topside charging their batteries.

Everyone on the USS Endymion was very still and quiet as we passed the Japanese's sub in the middle of the night in the thick fog.

To my surprise they passed us by without any incident because they could not see us in the thick fog.

The acting skipper took her off the zigzag course. It was foggy all that day and slightly that night. The fog cleared about the third day. Some of us did not have any idea as to where we were. I lost count of the days but after a couple of more days, we reached one of the islands off Eniwetak.

We were there for repairs on the public address, PA system, because it was knocked out when we were torpedoed.

Other ships in the harbor received the news that we were torpedoed and sunk. Everyone was glad to see us because they just knew we were down on the bottom of the ocean by now.

The USS Endymion was like a ghost ship. Every time someone saw her, they gasped and or prayed. It was indeed a miracle.

After a few days there we left for Pearl Harbor on a straight course, still steering by hand going six knots or less.

In the meantime, the United States dropped the first atomic bomb on Hiroshima.

The second bomb was dropped on Nagaski.

When we reached Pearl Harbor several days later the war was over.

And I was glad and thankful.

My knees ached for days from praying and kissing the ground.

We were at sea from the 7th of June 1945, not counting the short stay in Eniwetak for repairs, to early August 1945.

When we reached Pearl Harbor the captain was taken from the ship to some hospital, I guess.

The USS Endymion went into dry dock to repair the rudder, the after steering gear, and other damages that were sustain from the torpedo.

I had a time getting use to peace time in Pearl Harbor. It was nerve wrecking. Every time the PA system opens to pass the word, I began to run. Then I would remember that the war was over. We were in peace time and in port. It took weeks for me to get this right in my mind.

Other crew members felt the same way.

Members of our crew took turns going to a rest area for a week. We were really shaking up from the torpedo and with no connection to the outside world for days. That was a scary thing. We really needed the rest. We were in dry dock but the entire crew could not all go at the same time. So we took turns.

At the rest area we lay around and just rested from any duty on the ship and after a while a body relaxed and let out a lot of tension.

During my stay, I thought hard about the torpedo that hit the USS Endymion. And the fact that we were saved because the ship was on a roll when we were hit, then saved by an airplane that belonged to neither sides, and then saved by a thick fog.

I thought there we were waiting on the Japanese to open fire, and then suddenly a plane appeared. The Japanese thought it was ours and we thought it was theirs. If it were ours it would have fired on the Japanese, and if it were the Japanese they would have dropped bombs on us.

That was a mystery. Who did the plane belong to? Why was it out there so low? No one had any answers.

It was a mystery of the fog and how we hid for days without bumping into anything and getting safely home. I decided long ago both of these feats were acts of God.

God had protected us. I believe this and no one can tell me any differently. Even now when I think about those events, I shutter.

* * *

There was a big victory parade in Honolulu on August 14th when the Japanese surrendered. I went ashore and stayed all day.

Sailors and soldiers were everywhere.

I saw lots of fights on King and Hotel streets. I avoided them because my enlistment was nearing and I wanted to be careful not to get into any trouble.

There was a bulletin from the Navy department concerning men being discharged. They were setting up a point system. This point system totaling 44 points consisted of the amount of months a reservist had accumulated during his tour in the Navy. I did not need this 44 point system because my enlistment was soon to be up.

Being a short timer I told the mess caterer I would like to be relieved from cooking duties. He agreed. Short timers had it made.

I could get up when I wanted to eat breakfast. I had nothing to do but relax, rest, and go ashore. This was August 1945 and I was coming out in September 1945. That was less than a month away.

TOURS OF DUTY AND WAR WERE OVER
Chapter 10

"We are all in the same boat in a stormy sea and we owe each other a terrible loyalty."

G. K. Chesterton

At the end of the war my first enlistment was up and a decision had to be made: reenlist or come out. I was serving on the USS Endymion and I pondered the question of another hitch in the Navy. I knew that this racial problem was there and it would always be there. It would never go away, not in my lifetime anyway.

During the five Navy reserve cruises that I participated in for six years, I did not see any black midshipmen or any black Navy reservist from any of the colleges or any African-Americans on the cruises from officers' candidate school.

Yet Dorie Miller manned a 50 cal machine gun and shot down a Japanese plane or two proved that if African-Americans had been given the training like any other white sailor, instead of being confined to serving meals and making up bunks, the Navy for African-Americans would have been better. Seeking a career in the Navy as a mess attendant was not what I had in mind. But even as a mess attendant we did our best. Yet our best was not good enough.

I was being discharged and going out into a world quite different from what I had just experienced for six years. There was always a chance of going upstate where if I did not like the job or supervisor or men on the job, I could always walk away.

Finally I reached my decision, I was going out.

Informing the ship yeoman of my decision, I was offered my First Class rate back and chief cook. I lost my First Class rate on the USS Argonne because I refused to cook smelly meat.

In solitude, I asked myself,"Why wasn't I given my First Class rate back before now?"

Now it did not take long for me to see that I was being tricked into shipping over since I was regular Navy. No dice!

After being transferred to the receiving station and waiting transportation to the states for discharge, the day finally arrived.

Sailors, including me, were assembled on the tennis court for muster in Honolulu.

As names were called we loaded on to transport trucks that took us down to the docks to the troop transport ship. This group of men was scheduled for the south west area of the states.

After getting settled down and squared away on board the troop ship the captain piped for me on the mike to meet him in the mess room. Being the senior man among the mess attendants he put me in charge of feeding the officers. I was assigned the acting steward for the duration of the trip home to the states and the black seamen and other mess attendants were to serve the tables and to take orders from me and do whatever I assigned them to do.

I had orders from the captain of the ship that anybody, even officers, gave me trouble to report it to him.

And that was what I had intended to do, no more or no less.

* * *

An incident happened on the troop transport ship to San Pedro further convinced me that I was during the right thing about getting out instead of reenlisting.

The word was passed over the mike: "All officers being transferred to the states will eat in mid-ship mess room."

After I got a list of all officers from admiral to ensigns, seating was done according to seniority.

Everything was going well before dinner, when an officer, a Lieutenant Commander wanted to change the seating arrangements. He wanted to sit in another officer's seat at the table where twelve Army nurses were seated.

The Lieutenant Commander walked over to the ladies and pulled up a chair and began a seductive conversation with them. He was really enjoying their company.

I had assigned the twelve Army nurses that were also being transported to the states, to a middle table with other officers.

The Lieutenant Commander was asked his name and checking the list showed that he was supposed to sit on the first table and not at the middle table with the nurses but he refused to sit at the first table. He flatly refused to move. He was going to push me around and have his way. He did not want a mess boy giving him orders.

At first he and I starred each other down.

Finally he turned back to the nurses and picked up the conversation again with them and he just simply ignored me.

I could not tell him anything. I kept saying, "Sir, your seat is over here." He continued trying to talk to the nurses as if I was invisible.

They were half listening because they were waiting for him to obey orders or for me to give up and walk away.

But to no avail, we both held steadfast.

Finally I shouted orders to the mess attendants "Stop the chow, don't serve any more!"

The dinner was stopped and nothing was served. The mess room was very quiet. You could hear a rat walk on cotton.

After a long moment of silent, an admiral waved his arm in a becking manner to the officer, speaking to the officer jovially, "Hey sailor, come on over here and sit down."

As the officer stood up to leave, he gave me a long stare, and I braced myself for a fight to death.

The other mess fellows got scared and they knew that a killing was about to take place. But instead the Lieutenant Commander pushed the chair roughly away from him and went to his assigned table and sat down.

Everyone breathed a sigh of relief, including me, although I decided a long time ago that I was not letting anyone push me around any more. I knew dogs that got better treatment. In addition I knew the captain would back me up.

I gave orders to continue serving. After dinner, that officer gave me a real mean look, letting me know if I were not going out, I would be in deep water.

For five days from Honolulu to San Pedro we mess attendants served officers chow in the mid-ship mess room without any more trouble. They stayed out of my way and I stayed out of theirs.

* * *

DISCHARGING

"There is nothing by which men display their character so much as in what they consider ridiculous."

Goethe

After reaching San Pedro, the sailors that were scheduled for the southwest area boarded the troop train for the long ride to Camp Wallace near Galveston via Houston. We had a three hour lay over in Houston. Most of us fellows from Houston went home to our families for the lay over.

Upon arriving at the discharge center we were briefed several days about benefits, VA, VFW, and given medical examinations. The waiting period began.

The day came and it took almost three hours to complete the discharged process. Our personal things were issued in one area and we were interrogated in another area. A lot of our personal things and souvenirs were missing when we received them at the exit gate because of the manner the Navy discharged us.

We were given bus fare from Camp Wallace back to our destination.

I was discharged six years and one month to the day – September 18, 1939 to October 18, 1945.

* * *

After being discharged I felt lost in Houston. It was kind of hard for me to adjust for a day or two.

I was promised a job in Ohio, railway mail, and after being around home for a little while and unable to adjust to southern ways knowing what I had been through, I decided to leave and go upstate.

As the train rolled on north, looking out of the window at the fields and vast open space, I thought about how I would make it upstate.

But as the train rolled on, quietness settled in and sleep overcame my thoughts.

I was resting comfortable in a nice warm seat for the moment and all of my worries were over. I thought!

Sylvia Johnson-Cooper, a Reading Specialist, has a PhD in Philosophy. This is her first nonfiction. Her first short story is called "***Goat Milk, Garlic, Goobers, Gumbo, Gals, Guys, and God: True Confession Is Good for the Soul***" She is currently working on her third book, "Si***sters from the Start***". Johnson-Cooper has two sons and three grandchildren. She lives in Darby Hill, Texas.

* * *

Roosevelt "Rosy" Flenard, a Church of Christ ordained minister, lives with his wife Betty in Columbus, Ohio. He is a retired postal carrier.

Send all correspondence to:

72 Holiday Village
Pointblank, Texas 77364

Printed in the United States
102189LV00001B/130-423/A